The Prudential
Financial Planning Guide

The Prudential Financial Planning Guide

by *The Prudential Insurance Company of America*

Katherine Barrett

Editorial Consultant

Collier Books
Macmillan Publishing Company · *New York*

Macmillan Publishing Company
866 Third Avenue, New York, N.Y. 10022

Library of Congress Cataloging in Publication Data
Main entry under title:
The Prudential financial planning guide.
  Includes index.
  1. Finance, Personal. I. Barrett, Katherine.
II. Prudential Insurance Company of America.
HG179.P74   1985   332.024   85-471
ISBN 0-02-008210-X

Macmillan books are available at special discounts for bulk
purchases for sales promotions, premiums, fund-raising, or
educational use. For details, contact:

Special Sales Director
Macmillan Publishing Company
866 Third Avenue
New York, N.Y. 10022

10 9 8 7 6 5 4 3 2

Printed in the United States of America

Foreword

Financial planning sounds very complex, but it's basically nothing more than managing your money to accomplish your goals.

Admittedly, there are very complex aspects to financial planning. Tax laws, for example, are intricate and frequently changing, and insurance and investments offer a bewildering array of choices. But the principles of managing your money are simple and relatively unchanging. This book is dedicated to helping you understand those principles —in the context of your own financial situation.

How do you deal with the complexities? If you are like most people, you use financial specialists, such as accountants, attorneys, insurance representatives, or securities brokers. However, *you* still have to make the decisions. *You* still have to understand the principles and know enough about the alternatives to obtain the greatest benefit from your specialists.

This book is designed to be easy to use. The text is lively and straight to the point. The worksheets help you get a clear understanding of your financial situation. Then, using checklists, you decide what you want to do. These checklists, together with your budget, constitute your overall financial plan. The only thing left is for you to pick up the phone, contact your financial specialists, and begin to implement your plan.

Joseph J. Melone

President
The Prudential Insurance
Company of America

Contents

Introduction

Don't be afraid of your money. It's there to help you—not to keep you awake at night. And while, at first glance, the financial world may look stupendously complex, it really isn't. With a little reading, figuring, and planning, you can make the right choices for yourself and your family.

One of the most positive developments in personal finance is that there are so many choices to make. More options bring more opportunities. And that means that you'll have no trouble tailoring a plan to meet your needs.

Not too many years ago the situation was much simpler. You could put your money into a savings account and feel superior to people who were still stuffing their money into mattresses.

Then came a series of changes that left the financial system in the United States forever altered. Interest rates, which used to move half a percent at a time, at most, began to rocket up and down like missiles. Inflation hit double digits, and then plummeted. These factors, combined with the partial deregulation of banks and other financial institutions, brought hundreds of new investment possibilities to the average person.

At the same time, people became better informed. They realized that the decisions they made about budgeting, credit, taxes, insurance, and retirement planning could affect the quality of their lives—today and in the future. And they began to understand that no decision could be made in a vacuum. The secret of financial planning is to look at the total picture.

Of course, for the average person who doesn't find balancing a checkbook a fun activity for a Saturday night, all these changes present something of a challenge: How do you put your financial house in order, without turning into a full-time financial housekeeper?

This book is the answer to that question. It gives you the tools so that with a little time and effort you can get a clear picture of your entire financial situation. It examines each of the major areas—goals, credit, taxes, insurance, investments, retirement planning, and budgeting—and helps you decide for yourself what you need to do in those areas.

Most important, this book does not get bogged down in technical details. It purposely avoids compound interest tables, discounted cash flows, and the usual jargon of the financial world, because most people are not interested in them. They depend on financial specialists—such as accountants, attorneys, insurance representatives, and securities brokers—to handle the more complex areas of their finances.

What most people want, instead, is the big picture—a clear idea of their financial needs so they can ask the right questions of their financial specialists. That's what this book is about—providing you with the tools to devise an overall financial game-plan that accomplishes what you want to do.

Remember, don't let your money control you; you should control your money. And maybe have a little fun doing it.

Chapter One

Getting Organized

Papers You Need to Get Started

It will be helpful to assemble a number of documents so you'll be able to find the information you'll need quickly and easily. In order to use this book most effectively—and to really understand your financial situation—you'll probably want the following:

1. Your most recent paycheck stub.
2. Records of your expenses for the last twelve months, including cancelled checks or checkbook registers.
3. Credit card bills for the last twelve months.
4. Bank statements, both checking and savings.
5. Your investment records.
6. Last year's tax returns.
7. Your individual insurance policies (life, homeowners, auto, etc.).
8. Group insurance policies or descriptive booklets.
9. Company pension information. (If you don't have this, it should be readily available from your company.)
10. Your yearly principal statement about your mortgage as well as your latest mortgage bill.
11. Loan agreements.
12. Child support or alimony papers.
13. Your will.
14. Household inventory—how much your valuables are worth.

Setting Up Your Files

Have you ever frantically searched your home for hours for a receipt or an old tax form or some other small remnant of a financial transaction?

There's no question that in financial planning, organization pays off. But the specifics of how you organize your files are really unimportant. Some people feel comfortable with shoeboxes in their clothes closet, while others have meticulously ordered file cabinets. The important thing is that you—and other members of your family—are able to find what you need easily.

In any event, here are a few tips to keep in mind.

1. Pick out one centralized place, such as a filing cabinet or several desk drawers, for the financial papers you regularly use: loan information, current bills, etc.

2. Make sure you have a safe but easily accessible place for those documents that you refer to irregularly but may need on short notice

RECORD TIMETABLE

DOCUMENT	WHERE TO KEEP	HOW LONG TO RETAIN
Birth certificate, marriage license, and divorce papers	Safe deposit box	Indefinitely
Military service records	Safe deposit box	Indefinitely
Vehicle titles	Safe deposit box	Until sale or discard
Real estate deeds	Safe deposit box	Until transfer of property
Household inventory	Safe deposit box (with working copy at home)	Keep current
Will	Lawyer and safe deposit box	Indefinitely
Contracts	Lawyer and safe deposit box	As long as current
Home purchase and home improvement records	Home and safe deposit box	As long as you own the home or are rolling over its profits into new homes
Insurance policies	Home (with policy numbers in safe deposit box)	Keep all life insurance policies, but otherwise retain only current policies
Stock or bond certificates	Broker	Until cashed in or sold
Investment purchase and sale records*	Home and broker	Six years after tax filing deadline in year of sale
Tax returns*	Home	Six years from filing date
Cancelled checks and bank statements*	Home	Six years
Receipts for large purchases	Home	Until sale or discard of item
Service contracts and warranties	Home	Until expiration
List of credit cards with account numbers	Home	Keep current

* Generally, the IRS will only audit you three years after filing, but it can go after large underpayments of tax as far back as six years and fraud indefinitely.

Names and Telephone Numbers of
Your Financial Specialists

	NAME	TELEPHONE
Accountant or tax preparer	_____	_____
Attorney	_____	_____
Banker	_____	_____
Insurance representative Life and health	_____	_____
Home and auto (if different from life and health representative)	_____	_____
Securities broker	_____	_____
Trust officer	_____	_____
Other	_____	_____
Other	_____	_____
Other	_____	_____

(a list of your credit card numbers, for instance, your household inventory, or insurance policies). Consider using a metal fireproof box for such important papers so that you won't be caught short in case of a fire, flood, or other disaster.

3. Arrange a spot for "dead storage," records you don't generally need to refer to but which you need to keep for safety's sake (tax returns or old cancelled checks).

4. Keep a record of where you keep your records. Make sure your family knows where this general inventory of documents is so that they can easily reach all your important papers in an emergency. Make a list of the names and phone numbers of any financial specialists who have assisted you, such as your accountant, your attorney, your insurance representative, or your securities broker. (See above.)

5. Accept the fact that you don't have to save everything. Some people are so cautious they end up keeping records that stretch back to the Hoover administration. In most cases, such a conservative approach is unnecessary.

6. Get a safe deposit box at the bank for records that are irreplaceable or extremely difficult to replace. But remember that in many states, entry to these boxes may be temporarily forbidden on the owner's death, so don't keep anything in them that your heirs may need to get to quickly (such as burial instructions or insurance policies).

The table on page 2 will help you decide where to keep some of your important papers and how long you need to keep them.

Your Will

It can't be said too many times: You should have a will. If you neglect to draw up a will, you greatly increase the cost to your heirs of settling your estate. In addition, you may lose all control over the disposition of your assets.

When you do have a will drawn up, and anytime you want revisions made, have a lawyer do it. The fee is really a small investment for the guarantee that your wishes will be carried out.

Remember, too, that after the will has been written, you still can't tuck it in a drawer and forget about it. You must keep it up-to-date. Here's a quick checklist of items that may make it necessary for you to have your will revised.

But before you get started, fill in here the date when your will was last reviewed:

_____

Now ask yourself these questions. If your answer to any of them is yes, you may want to consult your attorney.

Since you last reviewed your will:

1. Has there been any change in your marital status?
2. Have any of your heirs gotten married, divorced, had children, or died?
3. Have you added another dependent—either a child, an aging parent, or a relative with special needs for whom you have some responsibility? Would you want to provide for this person in your absence?
4. Have you inherited or otherwise acquired any large pieces of property?
5. Have you moved to a different state, which may have different laws for inheritance?
6. Have you acquired any property in another state?
7. Have you made any changes in your life insurance?
8. Has there been any reason to change the person named as executor or trustee in your will?

9. Has the value of your estate increased or decreased dramatically?

10. Has there been any major change in the tax laws that could save or cost you money?

Do you feel the need to review (or write) your will?

Yes ——————— No ———————

Your Income

The first important step in making sense out of your finances is to know how much money is coming in now. This isn't hard at all. In fact, if your financial status hasn't changed much, you may be able to take the figure from last year's tax form.

But if your situation has changed at all since last year—or if you simply want to get a good feel for your various sources of income and how important they are to you—just fill out the worksheet on page 6.

Some of the figures should be very easy to find—they'll come off such things as your paycheck stubs or the monthly statements from your broker. Another source of information is your own checkbook register. Try to use all current numbers, but if that's not possible in all cases (as with bonuses from your place of work), then just use last year's figures. Don't worry about getting these numbers right to the penny.

Your Net Worth

The key indicator of your financial health is your "net worth"—the total value of everything you own, reduced by any liabilities outstanding. This is the number you want to keep track of from year to year to see how well you're doing financially.

Wealthy people frequently claim that they don't know how much money they really have. And they're not lying. It's not easy to figure out the accurate value of acres and acres of real estate, houses all over the world, and a number of closely held companies.

Well, at least that's one good reason not to be rich. For most people, the process of calculating net worth is a relatively simple one. Of course, there are still *some* difficulties. There's no way to know exactly how much a house is worth, for instance, until you sell it. But that shouldn't concern you. A close estimate will do perfectly well for the purposes of general financial planning. A figure for the value of your house or condominium might be found by asking a friendly realtor for an estimate. Or you can look in the newspaper to see what is being asked for similar homes in your area. Subtract a little from those figures (they're "asking prices," remember) and you should have an idea of what your house would fetch if you put it up for sale.

What's Coming in Each Year?

	YOU	SPOUSE	OTHER
Total Annual Salary:	$_____	$_____	$_____
Bonuses:	_____	_____	_____
Interest from:			
savings accounts:	_____	_____	_____
certificates of deposit:	_____	_____	_____
loans to others:	_____	_____	_____
bonds:	_____	_____	_____
other investments:	_____	_____	_____
Real estate rental:	_____	_____	_____
Dividends from investments (stock):	_____	_____	_____
closely held companies:	_____	_____	_____
Trust income:	_____	_____	_____
Child support or alimony:	_____	_____	_____
Social Security:	_____	_____	_____
Pension or profit sharing:	_____	_____	_____
Other sources:	_____	_____	_____
Other sources:	_____	_____	_____
Other sources:	_____	_____	_____
Total income:	$_____ +	$_____ +	$_____ =

$_____

Where Do You Stand?

The typical American household had a median income of about $25,000 in 1983. Where does your family fit in?

Percentage of households with income:

Over $50,000	13%
Over $35,000	30%
Over $25,000	49%
Over $20,000	61%
Over $15,000	72%
Over $12,500	78%
Over $10,000	84%
Under $10,000	16%

The next few pages contain worksheets to help you estimate your current net worth. For some of the items, like certificates of deposit, there is only one line provided. You may well have a number of certificates of deposit. Just add up the total and enter it. You might consider attaching an itemized list of these particular assets to keep a complete record.

Unfortunately, figuring out your net worth isn't just a matter of totaling up everything you own. In order to get a meaningful number, you have to sum up all your assets and then subtract all your liabilities. Here, there should be little need for estimating. The people from whom you've borrowed will be only too glad to tell you exactly how much you owe them.

If you are married, it is important to record in whose name the specific assets or liabilities actually appear. Simply circle H (husband), W (wife,) or J (joint) on the chart.

What You Have   Date as of: _____

FINANCIAL ASSETS

Cash in checking account	$_____	H	W	J
Cash in checking account	_____	H	W	J
Cash in savings account	_____	H	W	J
Cash in savings account	_____	H	W	J
Certificates of deposit	_____	H	W	J
Cash value of insurance policies (see p. 37)	_____	H	W	J
Account balance—defined contribution pension plans	_____	H	W	J
Account balance—profit-sharing plan	_____	H	W	J
Account balance—thrift plan	_____	H	W	J
IRAs	_____	H	W	J
401-K plans	_____	H	W	J
Other pension plans	_____	H	W	J
Trust funds	_____	H	W	J
Loans owed you	_____	H	W	J
Market value of investments	_____			
savings bonds	_____	H	W	J
annuities	_____	H	W	J
stocks	_____	H	W	J
bonds	_____	H	W	J
mutual funds	_____	H	W	J

FINANCIAL ASSETS

limited partnership
units _____   H   W   J

Other _____   _____   H   W   J

Other _____   _____   H   W   J

Other _____   _____   H   W   J

Total financial assets $_____

PERSONAL ASSETS   Date: _____

Your home $_____   H   W   J

Second home   _____   H   W   J

Other real estate   _____   H   W   J

Automobile or recreational
vehicle   _____   H   W   J

Automobile or recreational
vehicle   _____   H   W   J

Furniture and appliances   _____   H   W   J

Jewelry and furs   _____   H   W   J

Collections   _____   H   W   J

Other _____   _____   H   W   J

Other _____   _____   H   W   J

Other _____   _____   H   W   J

Total personal assets $_____

What You Owe

Date: _____

Mortgages	$_____	H	W	J
Automobile loan	_____	H	W	J
Automobile loan	_____	H	W	J
Installment debt (on furniture, appliances, etc.)	_____	H	W	J
Credit/charge card	_____	H	W	J
Credit/charge card	_____	H	W	J
Credit/charge card	_____	H	W	J
Credit/charge card	_____	H	W	J
Bank/finance company loans	_____	H	W	J
Bank/finance company loans	_____	H	W	J
Life insurance loans	_____	H	W	J
Education loans	_____	H	W	J
Education loans	_____	H	W	J
Investment liabilities	_____	H	W	J
Other _____	_____	H	W	J
Other _____	_____	H	W	J
Other _____	_____	H	W	J
Total liabilities	$_____			

And the Result?

Now that you've figured out your total financial assets, total personal assets, and total liabilities, you are just two short steps away from an estimate of your total net worth.

First, add together your total financial assets and your total personal assets.

FINANCIAL ASSETS	$_____
PLUS	
PERSONAL ASSETS	$_____
	_____
TOTAL ASSETS	$_____

Then, subtract your total liabilities from your total assets to obtain your net worth.

TOTAL ASSETS	$_____
MINUS	
TOTAL LIABILITIES	$_____
	_____
NET WORTH	$_____

This is the ultimate measurement of your financial progress from year to year. If you really want to see how well you are doing, you should do this exercise every year or so. Then, by comparing your net worth from year to year, you can easily plot your financial growth.

If your net worth this year turns out to be negative, don't despair. A fair number of Americans owe more than they have, and this doesn't mean that disaster is at your doorstep.

It does, however, mean that you may want to pay particular attention to the chapters on goal-setting and budgeting.

Chapter Two

Goals

Thinking About the Future

Everyone likes to fantasize about a wonderful future. But daydreaming, while pleasant, doesn't usually get you very far. Turning dreams into reality requires careful planning.

This chapter is primarily concerned with savings goals. Of course, these are not the only important items on your financial agenda. Adequate insurance protection is an important goal. Reducing taxes and increasing investment income are important goals. But savings do play a big role in planning for the future—and making it the kind of future you'd like.

What do you really want out of the coming years? Listed on the facing page are a few of the most common savings goals. But you may have your own ideas. So have fun thinking about the things you really want out of life. This is your chance to dream a little bit and then to take your dreams one step toward fulfillment.

If you wish, sit down with your family and talk about the future. Goals are not solitary affairs; they can be events that the entire family will have to work toward—perhaps by forgoing other, current pleasures. But the entire family will generally be able to reap the benefits of the savings, either directly, as with a new house or car, or vicariously, as with your children's college education.

As you consider major future goals, you should try to make two important estimates: How much is the goal going to cost? And how soon do you want to reach it?

For purposes of this exercise, state the cost in *today's* dollars.

Adding It All Up

Now that you have some idea what your major goals are, you need to figure out exactly how much money you want to save in the year to come. As the sages say, a trip of a thousand miles begins with one step. In financial planning, a goal of many years begins with the first month.

You may be wondering how you take inflation into account. One

YOUR GOALS	AMOUNT	DATE NEEDED
Buying or remodeling your house (down payment plus closing costs, or cost of remodeling)	$_____	_____
Children's education (cost per year in today's dollars times number of years of school needed)		
Child 1	_____	_____
Child 2	_____	_____
Child 3	_____	_____
Child 4	_____	_____
Emergency fund (suggestion: at least three months of after-tax income)	_____	_____
Retirement fund (see chapter seven)	_____	_____
Other _____	_____	_____
Other _____	_____	_____
Other _____	_____	_____
Other _____	_____	_____

method is to use today's dollars in all calculations. This requires two assumptions: first, that any money saved is invested and earns interest at exactly the same rate as inflation, and second, that your income also increases at the same pace as inflation. These conservative assumptions will simplify your planning by avoiding the use of compound interest tables.

So, for example, if you want to have a $10,000 emergency fund saved in five years, you will divide the $10,000 by five and come up with a total of $2,000 a year. Of course, during each of those five years that amount may increase, as the cash needed for the emergency fund increases with inflation and your income, but the $2,000 is a solid figure for the first year.

Which brings up an important, and now obvious, point: You should go through the exercises in this book on a yearly basis in order to keep your goals and savings projects up to date.

To begin, simply fill out the following worksheet with the appropriate information and do a little math. Then you'll be ready for chapter eight, where you will actually calculate your budget for next year with your goals in mind.

You may discover that your savings goals are more than your budget can handle. In that case, you'll want to modify your goals or your budget in accordance with what you think is important. The key idea is to consider your savings goals *before* you budget, rather than just saving whatever is left after expenses. Think of your savings as money you pay *yourself*, before you pay the rest of your obligations. And pay yourself first.

YOUR GOAL	DATE NEEDED	TOTAL AMOUNT NEEDED TO BE SAVED		NUMBER OF YEARS *		AMOUNT TO BE SAVED FIRST YEAR
Home	_____	$_____	÷	_____	=	$_____
Education						
Child 1	_____	_____	÷	_____	=	_____
Child 2	_____	_____	÷	_____	=	_____
Child 3	_____	_____	÷	_____	=	_____
Child 4	_____	_____	÷	_____	=	_____
Emergency Fund	_____	_____	÷	_____	=	_____
Retirement	_____	_____	÷	_____	=	_____
Other _____	_____	_____	÷	_____	=	_____
Other _____	_____	_____	÷	_____	=	_____
Other _____	_____	_____	÷	_____	=	_____
Other _____	_____	_____	÷	_____	=	_____
Other _____	_____	_____	÷	_____	=	_____

Total amount to be saved first year   _____

* This is the number of years from today until the date needed.

Chapter Three

Borrowing and Credit

Many centuries ago, Shakespeare advised that you should "neither a borrower nor a lender be." Well, the Bard of Avon was a great writer, but he wasn't living in twentieth-century America. Today, borrowing and credit is a part of our day-to-day life—from the fifty cents a ten-year-old borrows for an ice cream cone to the tens of thousands of dollars you borrow to buy a house.

Borrowing is an important part of investing, usually referred to as "leverage." For example, investors often borrow money from a broker ("buying on margin") to buy more stock. If the investment works out well, the investor can get a greater return than he or she otherwise would have. Of course, if the stock goes down, the investor must still repay the borrowed money.

The ability to make purchases sooner, or use leverage, has a cost: interest. How much you actually pay for the privilege of borrowing money varies from debt to debt, but in all cases it's an extra expense. Fortunately, if you do borrow money, the government helps you out a bit by allowing you to deduct the interest charges—provided you itemize deductions. So, the higher the tax bracket you are in, the more that interest deduction is worth to you. Unfortunately, even if your interest is deductible for tax purposes, it still costs you money. And it's all too easy to get in debt over your head. The message is this: All borrowing should be done in moderation. If you borrow, do it wisely.

Your Debt and Its Cost

Back in chapter one you recorded and added up your total liabilities in order to calculate your net worth. Unfortunately, those liabilities don't just serve to keep your net worth down, they are also a drag on your income.

As a result, it may be instructive to go through your debt obligations one at a time. Look at how much you actually owe and how much interest you are paying. Then find your total debt, your annual interest payments, and your total monthly payments. These numbers may surprise you. Finally, it's a good idea to look at your monthly debt obligations (excluding your mortgage) and see what percentage of your monthly take-home pay they represent. If this percentage is too high, it indicates that you may be getting in over your head.

In filling out the worksheet on the facing page, you may need to refer to a number of documents. You should have your monthly bills available, especially your credit card bills. Last year's interest notices from banks and credit companies will help you to see how much you paid out last year in interest charges.

A few additional points before you go on with this worksheet:

- Precision is not crucial in an exercise like this one. Don't take time trying to come up with figures that are exact to the penny.
- When asked to fill in the current monthly payments on your charge cards, use the minimum monthly payment as shown on your most recent bill.
- If you have more of a specific kind of debt than the lines provided permit (four credit card debts, say), use the "other debt" lines at the end of the worksheet.
- If you don't have some of the information requested, or if some of the information doesn't apply to particular bills, don't worry about it. Just leave those lines blank.
- If some of your payments are not made on a monthly basis, divide by the appropriate number of months to convert to a monthly figure.

Now that you've gone through the work of recording and adding up your debt obligations, you can analyze those figures a bit. First of all, scan down the interest rate column. You may never have realized that some of your credit cards were charging quite that much interest. Then, look at how many months remain on your major obligations. Will you finish paying off anything soon?

Next, see how your actual monthly payments relate to your monthly take-home income.

$$\frac{\text{TOTAL MONTHLY PAYMENTS (excluding mortgage)} \quad \$\underline{\hspace{1.5cm}}}{\text{MONTHLY TAKE-HOME INCOME (average)} \quad \$\underline{\hspace{1.5cm}}} = \underline{\hspace{2cm}} = \underline{\hspace{2cm}}\%$$

YOUR DEBTS	TOTAL DEBT	INTEREST RATE	NUMBER OF MONTHS REMAINING	ANNUAL INTEREST CHARGE (last year)	CURRENT MONTHLY PAYMENT
Auto loan	$_____	_____	_____	$_____	$_____
Auto loan	_____	_____	_____	_____	_____
Appliances and furniture	_____	_____	_____	_____	_____
Credit card	_____	_____		_____	_____
Credit card	_____	_____		_____	_____
Credit card	_____	_____		_____	_____
Insurance loan	_____	_____		_____	_____
Bank loan	_____	_____	_____	_____	_____
Bank loan	_____	_____	_____	_____	_____
Education loan	_____	_____	_____	_____	_____
Education loan	_____	_____	_____	_____	_____
Finance company loan	_____	_____	_____	_____	_____
Finance company loan	_____	_____	_____	_____	_____
Other _____	_____	_____	_____	_____	_____
Other _____	_____	_____	_____	_____	_____
Other _____	_____	_____	_____	_____	_____
Other _____	_____	_____	_____	_____	_____
	$_____ Total debt			$_____ Annual interest charge	$_____ Total monthly payments

Where to Draw the Line

Although you must decide for yourself how much credit you can handle, credit counselors generally advise that your monthly debt obligations should be no more than 20 percent of your take-home pay, and preferably no more than 15 percent. (This figure excludes mortgage payments.) If you are concerned that you might have more debt than you should, later sections in this chapter should be of some assistance.

Are You In Over Your Head?

While rules of thumb can be helpful, you can generally tell if you've gone credit crazy without even picking up a calculator.

Here are a few questions about your use of credit. If you find yourself answering yes to more than a few of them, you may want to start rethinking your use of loans and credit cards.

1. Do you find yourself worrying about money frequently?
2. Are you getting deeper into debt each month?
3. Do you regularly find yourself near the limit on your credit cards?
4. Are you getting dunning letters from creditors?
5. Are you negotiating new repayment schedules with creditors?

The Road Back

If you feel your debt has gotten out of hand, don't despair. There are a number of techniques that will help you get things back under control. Some of them may be a bit painful, especially if you are a confirmed spendaholic. But they work.

1. First of all, you have to start paying off your debts. This means whittling down the *principal* on your loans and credit card bills, little by little, each month—not merely paying off enough interest to keep the wolves at bay.

2. To do that, you have to cut back on spending. You'll never get your debt load down if you keep spending more than you can afford every month. Put yourself on a credit card diet. Lock them in a drawer. Hide them from yourself. If you can't stay away, seize a rational moment and cut them to pieces.

3. Even as you are trying to pay off your bills, redouble your efforts to save a little money. As you pay off each debt, you'll find that you are able to save more and more.

4. Try to pay for new acquisitions with cash. For some people, spending with a credit card is like getting a free gift. But there's no such thing as a free gift in the world of borrowing. If you force yourself to pay with cash, you may just harness some of your excess spending.

5. Let your creditors know you are trying to pay off your bills. Set up a schedule you can meet. Most lenders are patient with borrowers who are making a good faith effort to pay them back.

6. If all else fails, seek credit counseling. The nonprofit Consumer Credit Counseling Services have offices in over two hundred cities around the country. One of their credit counselors will work with you to set up a workable budget that will allow you to pay off your debts. Generally, this service is performed without charge or for a nominal fee.

If there's no CCCS office in your area, there may be another low-cost financial counselor. Failing that, you might consider going to a commercial financial counselor, who will charge for the same basic services.

Chapter Four

Tax Strategies

Tax Planning and You

Uncle Sam needs money to run the government and he's going to get part of it from you. That's the bad news. The good news is that with a little thought and planning, it may be possible to lessen your tax bill significantly—thus giving you more money to spend where you'd like.

There's nothing immoral or illegal about tax planning. In fact, most of the ways you can lessen your tax bill were designed by the government, which uses tax breaks to encourage certain kinds of behavior. The tax benefits associated with owning a house, for example, are in place because the federal government wants to encourage private ownership of homes.

In any case, remember the quote from the famed jurist, Judge Learned Hand: "Over and over again, courts have said that there is nothing sinister in so arranging one's affairs as to keep taxes as low as possible. Everybody does so, rich or poor, and all do right, for nobody owes any public duty to pay more than the law demands."

Your Tax Bracket

The phrase "tax bracket" is central to tax planning, yet you'd be surprised how many people don't know what bracket they're in.

Tax bracket refers to your marginal tax rate—the rate you would pay on the next dollar of income. It does *not* refer to your overall tax rate.

So, for example, in 1984, if you and your spouse, filing jointly, had between $35,200 and $45,800 of taxable income, then you would be expected to pay $6,274 on the first $35,200 of this taxable income. That works out to an overall rate of only 17 percent. But everything you made in excess of $35,200 would be taxed at a 33 percent rate. That 33 percent is called your marginal tax rate or tax bracket.

On the following pages are some tables that will help you to see which tax bracket you are in. These numbers are based on 1984 IRS tables; obviously, they will change from year to year.

To use these tables, simply find your appropriate filing status (married or single, for example), and your taxable income.

Write your tax bracket here:

_____%

1984 IRS Tax Tables

Single Individual

IF YOU EARN BETWEEN (TAXABLE INCOME)	YOU'LL PAY	ON THE FIRST	AND THIS MARGINAL TAX RATE ON THE REST
$2,300–3,400	0	$2,300	11%
$3,400–4,400	$121	$3,400	12%
$4,400–6,500	$241	$4,400	14%
$6,500–8,500	$535	$6,500	15%
$8,500–10,800	$835	$8,500	16%
$10,800–12,900	$1,203	$10,800	18%
$12,900–15,000	$1,581	$12,900	20%
$15,000–18,200	$2,001	$15,000	23%
$18,200–23,500	$2,737	$18,200	26%
$23,500–28,800	$4,115	$23,500	30%
$28,800–34,100	$5,705	$28,800	34%
$34,100–41,500	$7,507	$34,100	38%
$41,500–55,300	$10,319	$41,500	42%
$55,300–81,800	$16,115	$55,300	48%
Over $81,800	$28,835	$81,800	50%

Unmarried Head of Household
(if you are providing over half the support for qualifying relative)

IF YOU EARN BETWEEN (TAXABLE INCOME)	YOU'LL PAY	ON THE FIRST	AND THIS MARGINAL TAX RATE ON THE REST
$2,300–4,400	0	$2,300	11%
$4,400–$6,500	$231	$4,400	12%
$6,500–8,700	$483	$6,500	14%
$8,700–11,800	$791	$8,700	17%
$11,800–15,000	$1,318	$11,800	18%
$15,000–18,200	$1,894	$15,000	20%
$18,200–23,500	$2,534	$18,200	24%
$23,500–28,800	$3,806	$23,500	28%
$28,800–34,100	$5,290	$28,800	32%
$34,100–44,700	$6,986	$34,100	35%
$44,700–60,600	$10,696	$44,700	42%
$60,600–81,800	$17,374	$60,600	45%
$81,800–108,300	$26,914	$81,800	48%
Over $108,300	$39,634	$108,300	50%

Married Individuals Filing Joint Return or Surviving Spouses

IF YOU EARN BETWEEN (TAXABLE INCOME)	YOU'LL PAY	ON THE FIRST	AND THIS MARGINAL TAX RATE ON THE REST
$3,400–5,500	0	$3,400	11%
$5,500–7,600	$231	$5,500	12%
$7,600–11,900	$483	$7,600	14%
$11,900–16,000	$1,085	$11,900	16%
$16,000–20,200	$1,741	$16,000	18%
$20,200–24,600	$2,497	$20,200	22%
$24,600–29,900	$3,465	$24,600	25%
$29,900–35,200	$4,790	$29,900	28%
$35,200–45,800	$6,274	$35,200	33%
$45,800–60,000	$9,772	$45,800	38%
$60,000–85,600	$15,168	$60,000	42%
$85,600–109,400	$25,920	$85,600	45%
$109,400–162,400	$36,630	$109,400	49%
Over $162,400	$62,600	$162,400	50%

Married Individual Filing Separate Return

IF YOU EARN BETWEEN (TAXABLE INCOME)	YOU'LL PAY	ON THE FIRST	AND THIS MARGINAL TAX RATE ON THE REST
$1,700–2,750	0	$1,700	11%
$2,750–3,800	$115.50	$2,750	12%
$3,800–5,950	$241.50	$3,800	14%
$5,950–8,000	$542.50	$5,950	16%
$8,000–10,100	$870.50	$8,000	18%
$10,100–12,300	$1,248.50	$10,100	22%
$12,300–14,950	$1,732.50	$12,300	25%
$14,950–17,600	$2,395.00	$14,950	28%
$17,600–22,900	$3,137.00	$17,600	33%
$22,900–30,000	$4,886.00	$22,900	38%
$30,000–42,800	$7,584.00	$30,000	42%
$42,800–54,700	$12,960.00	$42,800	45%
$54,700–81,200	$18,315.00	$54,700	49%
Over $81,200	$31,300.00	$81,200	50%

Cutting Your Taxes

How can you reduce your taxes? Most of this chapter will focus on ways to cut your federal income tax. A brief section at the end discusses estate planning and the federal estate tax.

The most straightforward way to save on your annual tax bill is to take all the allowable deductions or credits. This is an area in which the law changes virtually every year, so it might be worthwhile to seek the help of an accountant or tax preparer. One additional significant deduction can easily pay his or her fee (which is deductible, too).

For financial planning purposes, however, it is necessary to take a long-range look at ways to reduce your tax burden. There are basically four strategies available: conversion, deferral, deflection, and deduction. Each has certain applications for which it is particularly well suited. As you read this section, ask yourself whether you are already using each of these strategies and whether you should consider doing so. A Tax Strategy Checklist at the end of the chapter will allow you to summarize your decisions.

Conversion

The first strategy for reducing your taxes is conversion, which applies to investment return. The idea is to convert investment return into money that will be taxed at lower rates than ordinary income, or not taxed at all.

Here are a few ways this can be done.

Capital Gains

One of the most important tax benefits the government gives investors is the opportunity to pay capital gains taxes on the profits from some long-term capital investments, instead of ordinary income taxes.

If a profit is taxed as a capital gain, then you pay only 40 percent of the rate you would have otherwise paid. So, someone in the 50 percent tax bracket paying a capital gains tax would pay only 20 percent of the profit (that's 40 percent multiplied by 50 percent). And no one can deny that a 20 percent tax is better than a 50 percent tax.

To qualify for long-term capital gain treatment, an asset must have been held at least six months if purchased on or after June 22, 1984, or at least twelve months if purchased before that date. That's why investors will often be careful to hold stocks for at least a minimum period before selling them at a profit.

As always, it's very important to keep accurate records of your investments to prove that they qualify for capital gains treatment.

Your Home

Owning your own home offers many tax advantages. The most obvious is the deductibility of mortgage interest and taxes. But the treatment of the appreciated value is equally important. It's a special case of capital gains treatment.

When you sell your current home and take a profit, Uncle Sam will look the other way as long as you use the money to buy another home within twenty-four months—what real estate people call "rolling over" the investment. You'll be able to put off paying any tax on the appreciated value of your old home as long as you keep getting more expensive ones.

What's more, if you are age fifty-five or older, the government provides for a $125,000 exclusion on the gain from the sale of a residence. This is a one-time benefit and only applies to the sale of your principal residence.

Finally, even if you are eligible for none of these tax savings when you sell your home—if, for example, you are selling at age thirty-five in order to move into a rental apartment—then the profits may still be taxed at the capital gains rate, instead of as ordinary income.

The result is that you will very likely *never* have to pay taxes on the appreciated value of your home. And if you do have to pay taxes, it will probably be at capital gains rates.

Municipal Bonds

Municipal bonds offer a way to receive tax-free income, especially useful for individuals in higher tax brackets. Of course, there's a trade-off for the tax-free status of such investments: They usually pay less interest than taxable bonds. You will have to figure out the after-tax return to you of both municipal bonds and other investments before you decide to take one route or the other. Remember, too, that the market value of municipal bonds, like that of all bonds, is subject to fluctuations caused by changes in interest rates.

Deferral

A second strategy for reducing your taxes is to defer them to future years, especially if you're saving toward retirement. By deferring taxes, you have the use of the money that would otherwise have gone to pay taxes and you can invest it to make more money. In addition, if you wait until after retirement to pay the taxes, you are likely to be in a lower income tax bracket, thus saving even more money.

There are two main types of tax deferral—deferral with after-tax dollars and deferral with pre-tax dollars.

Deferral with After-Tax Dollars

A good example of tax deferral with after-tax dollars is the deferred annuity (sometimes called a nonqualified annuity). Although the money you put into such an annuity is not tax-deductible, these long-term savings instruments do provide some excellent tax benefits.

Think of your annuity as an investment that works in two parts: the accumulation period, discussed in this chapter, and the payout period. During the accumulation period, while the annuity is earning money for you, you won't pay any taxes on the return.

To see just how dramatically this tax deferral mechanism can increase the return on your money, take a look at Diagram 1. The example illustrated is of two people in the 35 percent tax bracket who invest $1,000 at the same time, and each earns a 10 percent return. Over a thirty-year period, the tax deferred investment grows to about $17,400, while the taxed investment grows to only about $6,600.

Because this tax advantage is intended to encourage savings for retirement, however, a penalty is assessed against certain withdrawals prior to age fifty-nine and a half.

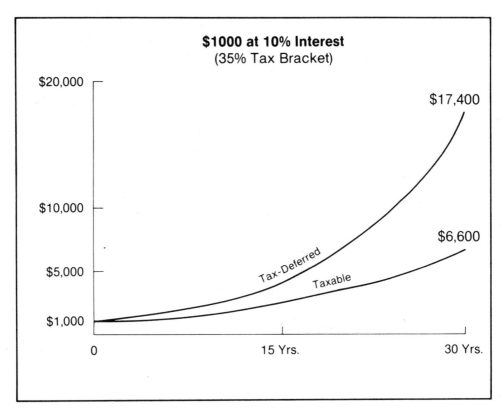

$1000 at 10% Interest
(35% Tax Bracket)

Diagram 1

A similar type of tax advantage is available if your employer offers a thrift plan. The earnings on such a plan accumulate with the same tax deferral. And some may allow you to withdraw certain amounts without penalty or taxation.

Deferral with Pre-Tax Dollars

An even more powerful tax advantage is offered by arrangements involving pre-tax dollars. The best known are Individual Retirement Accounts (IRAs), but 401-K plans and certain other plans utilize the same concept.

IRAs. Right now, Individual Retirement Accounts are an excellent way for many people to save toward retirement. They also present a rare opportunity to defer taxes on ordinary income.

IRAs allow you to contribute up to $2,000 of earned income per employed spouse (or $2,250 for an individual with an unemployed spouse) each year into a retirement fund. The amount you put in is deducted from your net income for purposes of calculating your yearly taxes. So, if you and your spouse had $31,000 of otherwise taxable income last year, and were able to put $4,000 into two IRAs, you would have paid taxes on only $27,000.

Since any income produced by an IRA investment will not be taxed until you take the money out, you'll be able to put your money in high-yielding taxable investments without worrying about Uncle Sam. And, since the taxes are deferred until you withdraw your savings at retirement, you'll probably pay taxes at a lower tax rate than the one you have now.

To see the difference that using pre-tax dollars makes, look at Diagram 2. It shows the same example used previously, of people in the 35 percent tax bracket depositing the equivalent of $1,000 in after-tax dollars and earning 10 percent a year for thirty years. But now the IRA grows to $26,800 instead of only $17,400. The difference? The starting amount is $1,538 pre-tax, which is the equivalent of $1,000 after-tax in the 35 percent bracket.

You can invest this money in almost any way you choose, such as in a bank account, insurance company annuity, mutual fund, or even in a self-directed brokerage account. But there is one caveat here: If you choose to break into the IRA at some point before you reach age fifty-nine and a half, the amount withdrawn is taxed as ordinary income and, in addition, there is a penalty equal to 10 percent of the total amount withdrawn (not just 10 percent of the interest).

But the tax savings from IRAs are so beneficial that even this drawback shouldn't stop you from setting one up. In fact, if you keep your

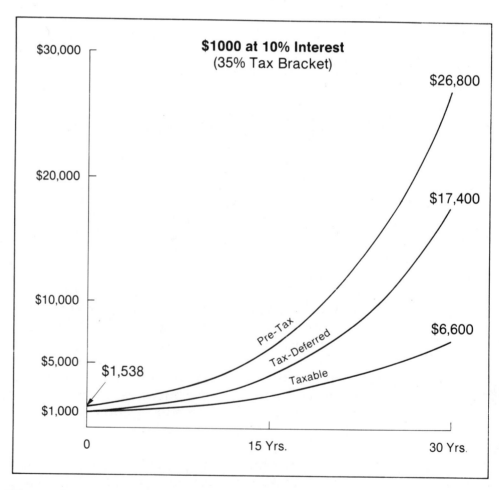

Diagram 2

money in the IRA for more than a few years, even these withdrawal penalties don't outweigh the benefits. The table below, prepared by Big-Eight accounting firm Deloitte Haskins & Sells, shows you how many years it takes before the tax benefits of putting your money into an IRA outstrip the penalties of taking money out before age fifty-nine and a half.

Years Required to Hold an IRA (After Penalty) For a Yield Greater Than a Taxable Investment

		Interest Rate on the IRA			
		8%	10%	12%	14%
		(number of years)			
	20%	9	8	7	6
Your tax bracket	30%	7	6	5	5
	40%	7	5	5	4
	50%	6	5	5	4

Keep in mind that if you are over age fifty-nine and a half, there is no penalty on withdrawals.

401-K Plans and Other Plans. Like IRAs, 401-K plans are excellent tax deferral arrangements. But since they are set up by employers, rather than individuals, not everyone has an opportunity to get involved.

If you *are* fortunate enough to have an employer who offers a 401-K plan, you should give it careful consideration. These plans, which can be used in addition to an IRA, allow you to reduce your taxable income each year by a certain amount and defer any taxes on it or the income it produces.

Some companies even take this a step further, and match their employees' contributions in some way.

When available, 401-K plans may offer several advantages over IRAs: contribution amounts may be larger, there is the possibility of "hardship" withdrawals prior to retirement without penalty, and lump sum distributions at termination of employment or retirement may qualify for a very favorable tax treatment called "ten-year forward averaging." (IRA withdrawals are always treated as ordinary income.) In addition, some 401-K plans allow loans. On the other hand, IRAs offer the ability to always withdraw your money prior to age fifty-nine and a half if you're willing to pay the 10 percent penalty plus any tax due. And IRAs are available to all wage earners. (Remember that even if you participate in a 401-K plan, you can still have an IRA as well.)

There are other plans that utilize the same concept of saving pre-tax dollars for retirement purposes. They include pension plans for self-employed individuals (formerly called Keogh plans) and special tax deferred annuities for employees of public schools and certain tax-exempt organizations.

Deflection

A third strategy for reducing your taxes is to have the taxes on certain investment income paid by someone in a lower tax bracket. This technique is commonly used to provide money for children's college educations. If investments are shifted in this way, the interest earned will be taxed at lower rates and more will be left when college rolls around. Here are some ways of using this technique.

Gifts to Minors

Each parent can give up to $10,000 a year to each child without incurring any liability for federal gift taxes. Once the money has been transferred to the child's account under the control of a custodian (not you), you no longer will have to pay any taxes on the income it generates; your child will pay at his or her tax rate.

The disadvantage here is that once your children reach legal majority, such as eighteen or twenty-one years of age (depending on the state), they can use their money however they'd like. You've made a gift and the money will never revert to you. If the legal age is twenty-one in your state, a simple gift under the Uniform Gift to Minors Act, as described above, should be sufficient to ensure that the money is used for college expenses. Another alternative is to set up a trust until your child is twenty-one. Consult your attorney if you're interested in these arrangements.

Low-Interest Loans

In years past, another way to deflect income was to make low-interest loans to children or other family members with lower tax brackets than your own. They could take in the income from those loans at their tax rates and then eventually repay the money to you.

However, the laws regarding these loans have recently changed. Within limits, it can still be a useful approach, but not as helpful as before. Consult your attorney for advice.

Clifford Trusts

If you want to use the income generated by certain assets to pay education expenses for your child, you might want to consider a Clifford trust. These trusts can be set up for you by a lawyer to help you to pay for your children's education in low-tax dollars. They work like this: You put money into a trust, which is simply a legal arrangement in which one person provides money for the benefit of another. However, the trust must be designed to last for at least ten years and one day. Then your child receives the benefit of the income from the investments in the trust and pays taxes on that income at his or her lower tax rate. At the end of the time, you get the principal back.

Such trusts can also be used to provide a steady stream of income for an aged parent. In this way, the parent will have the independence to use the income from the trust in any way desired, but you'll be assured of getting your principal back when the trust terminates (or if the beneficiary dies).

One warning: There may be some problems with Clifford trusts if you are a divorced parent paying a court-mandated amount for a child's college education. The IRS may feel that Clifford trusts cannot be used to discharge legal responsibilities.

Deduction

There are a number of available deductions that you can use on your tax form, as mentioned above. But there are also other, more complicated, ways of investing your money so that it actually generates deductions. This technique broadly applies to what people think of as "tax shelters."

A Word About Tax Shelters Generally

Most of the tax planning ideas considered so far have had little or no danger—an IRA, for example, is only as risky as the investments you choose for it. There are other ways that you can limit your tax bills, but they involve more risk. In general, these are dubbed "tax shelters," and you have to be very careful that they're not riddled with holes. They are also quite likely to trigger an IRS audit.

If someone suggested that you throw away $1,000 in order to save $500 in taxes, you'd think they were crazy. Well, some tax shelters fall into this category; they give you lots of tax deductions, but ultimately you come out the loser.

The idea that a tax shelter should have real economic benefits makes logical sense, but it's also a requirement of the Internal Revenue Service. If the IRS believes that a particular tax shelter was put together *only* for tax benefits, it may very well disallow those benefits.

Remember, too, that tax shelters are only for people with relatively high incomes. It doesn't make sense for someone in the 20 percent marginal tax bracket to forgo income in exchange for tax breaks—the breaks just don't make enough of a difference. In addition, many tax shelters have minimum net worth requirements of $100,000 or more that must be met before you can invest in them.

Limited Part-
nerships

Many shelters fall into one broad category: limited partnerships. Most of these limited partnerships are either in real estate, oil and gas, or equipment leasing.

A very simple example will illustrate how these things work—no deal would actually be this straightforward, but it will serve to make the point: In this hypothetical case, you are a limited partner with an investment of $80,000 in a real estate syndication. You receive a share of the rent coming in (say, $2,000 a year) and that provides income on which you would ordinarily pay taxes.

But wait. These buildings are also depreciating—that is, they are losing value over time—and the government will allow you to deduct that depreciation and certain other expenses (say, $10,000 a year) from your income. That's where the tax savings come in. You will be able to shelter not only the $2,000 of income from this investment, but also another $8,000 ($10,000 − $2,000) of your income from other sources. Some of these deals are even structured so that you will get to deduct an amount greater than your investment.

Finally, when these buildings have been fully depreciated, they can be sold, hopefully at a profit. Much of that depreciation will then be taxed, but only at capital gains rates. The overall effect is to save you a considerable amount in taxes.

A rule of thumb: If the shelter offers you more than a two-to-one write-off, be especially careful. Changes made in the tax law in 1984 make high-write-off tax shelters a questionable vehicle for most investors.

In any case, tax shelters can be a very complex area of financial planning. Don't enter into one without carefully reading through the prospectus and consulting a financial adviser. Don't let your desire to keep money from Uncle Sam blunt your common sense.

Other Tax Planning Tips

The tax code of the United States is so complex and full of potential benefits and pitfalls that it's impossible for an entire book, much less a short summary, to provide all the information a taxpayer needs. However, here are a few additional tips that have general applicability and may help you when April 15 rolls around:

Income Shifting. Since you are taxed on the income you make before January 1 of a given year, it can sometimes be beneficial to shift income into the next year. If you are going to receive payment for some service in late December, it may be advantageous to arrange to be paid in the beginning of January. Then you'll have the use of that money for a full year before you have to pay taxes on it.

Expense Shifting. On the other hand, you might benefit by moving upcoming expenses into the current year. For example, if you are planning to make a charitable donation in January, think about giving the money in December and getting the current deduction.

One idea here that is frequently missed: If you pay state income taxes, it may be possible to prepay next year's taxes this year, before January 1. That way, you can deduct that money from your current year's federal income taxes.

Second Home. As long as you do not use a second home for personal use for fourteen days or more during the course of the year, the government may allow you to deduct many of the costs associated with the home. If, over the course of the year, you are able to rent out this second home for a decent period of time, the income from the rental, coupled with the allowable tax deductions, can make it a very lucrative investment. And, of course, if you own your second home long enough, the profit from its sale will qualify as a capital gain.

Timing Losses. If you have made money in the stock market in the past year, you may want to take some losses as well. The losses can cancel out the gains and save you taxes.

Deductions and Tax Credits. People frequently overpay on their taxes because they are unaware of simple deductions that the government allows them. The list of credits and deductions that are frequently missed starts with such items as charitable contributions, child care, business-related moving expenses, business-related education expenses, energy tax credits, sales taxes, and interest payments.

Estate Planning

If you're concerned about the taxes you pay while you're living, you might also want to be concerned about the taxes due when you die. The process of trying to reduce or eliminate those taxes is often called "estate planning." And the tax of particular interest is the Federal Estate Tax.

Fortunately (or unfortunately, depending on how wealthy you are), the Federal Estate Tax only affects people with big bucks. You should be concerned if your net estate might exceed $400,000 in 1985 or about $600,000 in 1987 and later. So the first question you want to ask yourself is whether your total net worth, including jointly owned real estate and death benefits payable from life insurance, puts you anywhere near this benchmark.

If so, you should seek expert advice. Estate planning is *not* a do-it-yourself operation. Usually, it involves at least three key people, who work as a team. Your attorney is vital not only to draw up your will, but also to set up trusts and handle any legal questions that arise. Your accountant and attorney will advise you on the complex tax questions involved. And a qualified life insurance representative is important because the purpose of estate planning is to provide for your family after the death of you or your spouse. However, you need an insurance representative with specialized training in estate planning, such as that usually indicated by the designation CLU (Chartered Life Underwriter). Qualified insurance representatives often coordinate the activities of the estate planning team because of their knowledge and experience in this area. Other specialists, such as securities brokers or trust officers, may be involved, depending on your circumstances.

What does estate planning involve? One main focus is liquidity—what money will be used to pay the estate tax, not to mention the state inheritance taxes and other probate expenses. If your assets are primarily in bank accounts, there is little problem. But if your assets are tied up in a business, or a farm, or other real estate, it may not be that easy to turn them into cash. This is the reason why life insurance is the solution to certain liquidity problems—it provides dollars at exactly the time they're needed.

Another main issue is reducing your estate tax burden; this is done using a variety of planning techniques. For example, you probably want to make full use of your exemption amount of about $600,000 (1987 and later). You may want to make tax-free gifts of up to $10,000 a year per recipient ($20,000 from you and your spouse) in order to reduce your net estate. And you need to carefully consider whether assets, such as real estate, should be held in your name, your spouse's name, or jointly.

The Federal Estate Tax can take a sizable chunk of money from your family. For example, if your taxable estate is valued at $1 million for Federal Estate Tax purposes and your spouse is deceased, Uncle Sam will take about $190,000, or 19 percent of the taxable estate. Anything you do to reduce the tax bite will provide that much more money to your family.

The key is planning. If you think you may be affected by the Federal Estate Tax, contact a professional with specialized training in this area.

Tax Strategy Checklist

The following list is a recap of all the tax planning ideas discussed in this chapter. Run through the list and check off those that are in use and any which you would like to explore further as tax planning devices.

TAX STRATEGY	CONCEPT	IN USE	WORTH PURSUING?
Federal Income Tax			
Conversion	Capital gains (p. 23)	————	————
	Home ownership (p. 23)	————	————
	Municipal bonds (p. 24)	————	————
Deferral	Annuities (p. 24)	————	————
	IRAs (p. 25)	————	————
	401-K plans (p. 27)	————	————
	Other plans (p. 28)	————	————
Deflection	Gifts to minors (p. 28)	————	————
	Low-interest loans (p. 28)	————	————
	Clifford trusts (p. 28)	————	————
Deduction	Ordinary deductions	————	————
	Tax shelters (p. 29)	————	————
Federal Estate Tax			
Estate Planning		————	————

Chapter Five

Insurance

Protecting Your Financial Resources

If you scrimp and save for years and then a sudden illness wipes out your savings, all your hard work goes down the drain. The fact is that you face many similar risks of financial loss in everyday life: you might die prematurely, you might become permanently disabled and unable to work, your home might burn down, your car might hit another car —or person. Insurance protects you against these risks, and others. It provides a secure foundation for the rest of your financial planning.

When you have a particular risk of loss and don't purchase insurance, you are "self-insuring." If the loss occurs, *you* suffer. For example, if you have a $100,000 house and leave it totally without insurance, you save the insurance premium of perhaps $400 a year. However, if the house burns to the ground you are out $100,000. Most people don't take that risk.

For financial planning purposes, you need to take a hard look at each of the following risks of loss. How does each one apply to your own situation? Your insurance representative can be very useful in evaluating these risks and in helping you prepare a program to meet your needs. But the ultimate decision is up to you. You have to decide how much insurance you need and how much you can afford. Remember, the risk, and ultimately the loss if one occurs, falls on you.

The first three of the following sections discuss life, disability, and medical care insurance. The last three deal with homeowners, automobile, and personal catastrophe coverage.

Life Insurance

What risk does life insurance protect against? Some people simply say, "Death." But it's really the *financial* loss caused by *premature* death. The reason for saying "financial" loss is that nothing can protect a family against the emotional loss caused by the death of a loved one. Many times, however, the emotional loss is magnified by the financial woes of the surviving family members. Experts also specify "premature" death because death at age one hundred rarely causes severe financial loss. Yet unexpected death at age thirty, or fifty, or even seventy, often does. Such a loss can be offset by the instant "wealth creation" provided through life insurance.

How Much Life Insurance?

The amount of life insurance to carry is a personal decision for you and your spouse. For financial planning purposes, you need to make a *rough* estimate of your needs so you know if your current coverage is in the right ballpark. The worksheet on page 36 does this in two steps. First, it calculates the economic value of your life (and your spouse's life) to your family by taking each person's total earned income and subtracting an amount for personal expenses and taxes. The remainder is what actually goes to your family—it's what your family would lose each year if that person died. The next step (multiplying by ten) converts this annual loss into the amount of life insurance needed, by taking Social Security survivor benefits, last expenses, inflation, and other factors into account.

CAUTION: This very rough estimate can't do justice to the many individual circumstances that can exist. If you have young children, aging parents who are dependent on you, or special liquidity needs at death, you may need more insurance. If you have no children or your children are grown, you may need less. Benefits paid by Social Security are greatly affected by the relative ages of your children and surviving spouse. For a more professional calculation tailored to your individual circumstances, you should contact an insurance representative for assistance.

Urgent Note to Business Owners

If you or your spouse own a business, there can be urgent business needs for life insurance in addition to the personal needs described here. A small business often falls apart after losing its key owner/employee, or there may be partnership or family disputes about the value of the business. Proper planning can avoid or minimize such disputes. Again, you'll probably want to consult an insurance representative on these needs.

Worksheet: Life Insurance Needs

	YOU	SPOUSE	CALCULATION EXAMPLE
1. Annual earned income (gross annual salary/ wages to nearest $1,000)	$_____	$_____	$30,000
2. Annual economic value to family (earned income [step 1] reduced by taxes and personal expenses [Simplified version —take 60 percent of #1])	$_____ *	$_____ *	$18,000
3. Multiply by ten (to obtain lump sum needed to generate such an income)	× 10	× 10	× 10
4. Rough estimate of life insurance needed	$_____	$_____	$180,000

* A homemaker who doesn't work outside the home has an economic value to the family conservatively estimated, in a recent survey, to average about $10,000 per year. Depending on functions performed and the number and ages of any children, the value may be substantially higher.

As was mentioned before, this is only a rough estimate. In fact, it essentially uses a formula of six times gross annual salary or wages. (Some experts prefer five times earnings or seven times earnings.) The reason for the two-step process (taking 60 percent, then multiplying by ten) is to help you understand exactly what is being protected by life insurance—the economic value of you and your spouse to the rest of the family unit.

Inventory of Life Insurance

Take a few minutes to prepare an inventory of the life insurance you and your spouse currently have so that you can compare it with the rough estimate of what you need, which you've just calculated.

Your Life Insurance

INSURANCE COMPANY	CASH VALUE	DEATH BENEFIT	BENEFICIARY
_____	$_____	$_____	_____
_____	_____	_____	_____
_____	_____	_____	_____
_____	_____	_____	_____
_____	_____	_____	_____
Total	$_____	$_____	

Your Spouse's Life Insurance

INSURANCE COMPANY	CASH VALUE	DEATH BENEFIT	BENEFICIARY
_____	$_____	$_____	_____
_____	_____	_____	_____
_____	_____	_____	_____
_____	_____	_____	_____
_____	_____	_____	_____
Total	$_____	$_____	

Be sure to include any group life insurance provided by your employer. Subtract the current value of any loan you've taken on a policy from the death benefit otherwise payable. Don't include extra death benefits payable in case of accidental death, if present.

Your Possible Need for Additional Life Insurance

Now find out if you possibly need additional life insurance by subtracting your current amount of insurance from the rough estimate of the total amount you need.

	YOU	SPOUSE
1. Rough estimate of life insurance needed	$_____	$_____
2. Current insurance	$_____	$_____
3. Possible amount needed (Step 1 minus Step 2)	$_____	$_____

Check here whether you feel your family's life insurance coverage is:

	YOU	SPOUSE
Adequate	_____	_____
Possibly inadequate	_____	_____
Definitely inadequate	_____	_____

Some Key Life Insurance Terms Defined

Term Insurance provides life insurance for a limited period of time—the "term." For example, if you purchase $50,000 worth of one-year term insurance and die during that one-year period, the insurance company pays $50,000 to your named beneficiary.

The premium rates for one-year renewable term insurance increase as you get older because the death rate increases—as shown in Diagram 3 for a twenty-five-year-old male.

Diagram 4 shows how the premium rates increase for five-year renewable term on the same twenty-five-year-old male. The rate stays the same for five years, then increases each time the policy is renewed.

Term insurance has one main advantage: It requires the smallest *initial* outlay. It provides the largest amount of coverage for a given premium. On the other hand, the premium increases as you get older and at some point becomes prohibitive. You normally have no cash value, and if you ever stop paying the premium the policy lapses and coverage ends. Term insurance is best suited for covering temporary insurance needs.

Permanent or Whole Life Insurance is usually designed to provide a premium that stays level. Because of this (see Diagram 5), the premium is higher than the one-year term premium in early years (A) and lower than the one-year term premium in later years (B). The excess in early

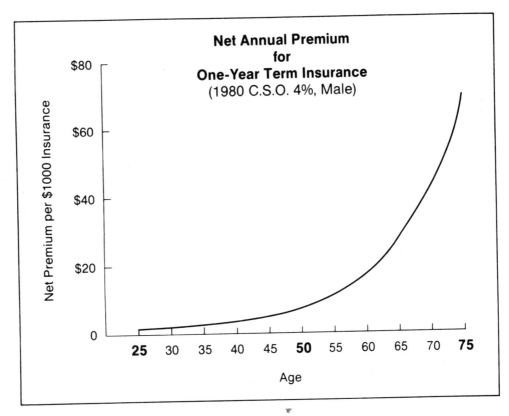

Diagram 3

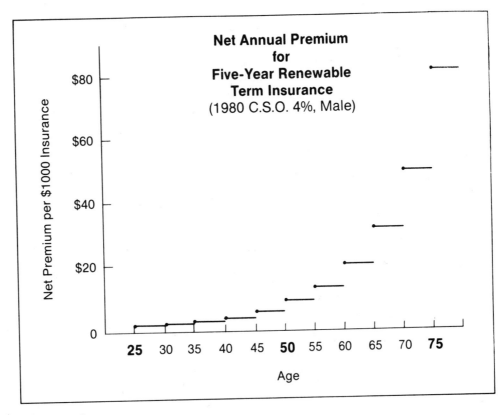

Diagram 4

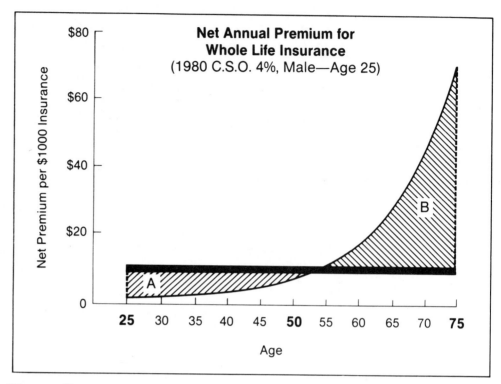

Diagram 5

years is accumulated, and after a few years serves to develop the cash value for the policy.

Permanent insurance offers several advantages. It provides lifetime insurance coverage at a premium rate that usually does not increase. It builds cash values that are "living" values, which may be very useful in an emergency or at retirement. They are available to you by taking a policy loan. And if you fail to pay a premium (due to oversight or a temporary financial bind) and the policy lapses, the basic coverage will usually remain in force for a certain period of time based on the cash value.

On the other hand, as stated, the initial premium rate for permanent insurance is higher than that for term insurance. The exact premium differential depends on the age and type of policy.

Participating Policies receive dividends, or more accurately "participate in the division of surplus." The premiums are set slightly higher than nonparticipating policies and part of the surplus at the end of each year, if any, is returned to the policyowner in the form of dividends. Thus, the net cost of the participating policy, including dividends, may be lower than the net cost of a nonparticipating policy. Any comparison of premium rates involving a participating policy should take dividends into account, because the dividends reduce the cost of the insurance.

Nonparticipating Policies do not receive dividends.

Riders can be added to custom-tailor your insurance policies by providing additional term insurance when you need it most or by including other benefits such as Waiver of Premium for Disability or the Accidental Death Benefit.

Settlement Options are different ways of receiving policy proceeds, usually including payment as a lump sum, receiving periodic payments for a fixed amount, fixed period, or as a lifetime income, or leaving the proceeds at interest. As policyowner, you may select the settlement option in advance or you may leave it to be chosen by the beneficiary. These options are important for planning purposes.

Variable Life Insurance provides the lifetime protection of traditional whole life insurance and allows you to direct the investment of the cash value into a common stock fund, a bond fund, a money market fund, perhaps a managed fund, or a combination of these funds. Premiums are level and the death benefit is guaranteed. The death benefit may increase if your investment choices are successful, but it can't decrease below the guaranteed amount. The cash value reflects the success of the underlying funds.

Universal Life Insurance places each of your premium payments into a "contract fund," which is invested in short or intermediate fixed income investments. When due, money is withdrawn from the contract fund to pay for insurance and certain policy expenses. The balance of the contract fund is used for the cash value.

Universal Life provides you with the flexibility to raise or lower your premium payments and sometimes the face amount of your policy within certain limits. Some premium payments can even be skipped completely. However, care must be taken not to reduce or skip too many premium payments. The contract fund must always be large enough to cover the cost of insurance and policy expenses when due, if the policy is to provide the lifetime protection of traditional whole life insurance.

Variable Universal Life Insurance is a combination of Variable Life and Universal Life. It offers the multiple funds approach of Variable Life (stock fund, bond fund, money market fund, etc.) with the flexibility of Universal Life. It's not yet widely available.

Replacement refers to the substitution of a new life insurance policy for an existing one. Such a replacement is rarely in your best interest, especially if your policy is the type that pays dividends. Any life insurance policy, whether term or whole life, incurs substantial expenses during the initial policy years. In buying a new policy, you would have to pay these initial expenses all over again, including the agent's commission. In addition, you may lose the ability to borrow at a favorable loan interest rate, as well as other valuable rights provided by the Incontestable clause and Suicide clause of the policy.

If you're asked to replace your life insurance, insist on a full and complete comparison (some states require this). For accurate information, make sure to notify the insurance representative or company that sold you the original policy.

Disability Income Insurance

If you're disabled so you can't work due to accident or sickness, your income stops. Disability income insurance can provide you with an income to replace at least part of what you were previously earning. The same type of coverage is available to your spouse if he or she is working.

Unfortunately, disability insurance is often neglected. People just assume they'll never be seriously disabled. But the probability of a serious disability (lasting 90 days or more) is actually much greater than the probability of death at most ages—and can be financially more disastrous. A working person who is totally disabled stops earning income for the family, just like one who dies, but in addition must still be provided with food and other necessities. Consider the financial hardship to your family if you (or your spouse) were totally disabled for a year. And then consider what would happen if that disability were permanent.

There are two types of disability coverage. Short-term disability provides for a relatively short disability benefit period, such as two weeks, thirteen weeks, twenty-six weeks, or one year. Long-term disability provides for longer disability periods, such as five years or to age sixty-five. Of the two, long-term disability is the more important and the most often neglected.

Many people have some disability income coverage on a group insurance basis through their employer. It may sometimes have a different name, such as "salary continuation." Always look first at your group disability coverage and then see if you need additional individual coverage to supplement it.

Your Current Disability Income Coverage

Several key terms affect your coverage and you need to understand them. In the blanks below write down what your current group or individual coverage provides.

Monthly Benefit Amount is the amount that will be paid to you if a disability (as defined in the policy) occurs. A typical group plan might provide 80 percent of your normal salary for six months. Some provide lesser amounts, such as 60 percent. Individual plans will rarely insure you for more than 60 percent of your normal income. Note that individual disability income benefits are usually exempt from federal income tax, so they should be compared to your after-tax income when working.

	YOU	SPOUSE
Your Monthly Benefit Amount or Percentage		
Short-term disability	_____	_____
Long-term disability	_____	_____

Benefit Period is the number of weeks or years for which benefits will be paid. This figure varies widely—it may be twenty-six weeks, fifty-two weeks, five years, or until age sixty-five. The longer, the better (and the higher the premium).

	YOU	SPOUSE
Your Benefit Period		
Short-term disability	_____ weeks	_____ weeks
Long-term disability	_____ years	_____ years

Waiting Period or Elimination Period is the number of weeks you must be disabled before benefits begin. (Benefits are not normally retroactive.) Short-term disability insurance usually has a short waiting period—three to thirty days. Long-term disability coverage tends to have a longer waiting period, such as six months or one year.

	YOU	SPOUSE
Your Waiting Period		
Short-term disability	_____ weeks	_____ weeks
Long-term disability	_____ weeks	_____ weeks

The Definition of Disability is obviously important, and there are several standard definitions of what constitutes disability:

1. "Unable to engage in any occupation": This is the strictest definition from the consumer's standpoint. Under this definition, if you can sell newspapers on the street corner, you're not disabled and shouldn't collect. Rarely used in policies issued today, but see the section on Social Security, page 44.

2. "Unable to engage in any occupation for which the insured is or becomes reasonably fitted by education, training, or experience": For example, a surgeon with a hand injury is not considered disabled if he or she can teach in medical school. Still a somewhat strict and limited definition.

3. "Unable to engage in own occupation": This is the most liberal definition. For example, the surgeon with a hand injury is considered disabled under this definition.

4. "Split definition": The modern trend is to combine 2 and 3, so the definition reads "Unable to engage in own occupation for two years" (the most liberal definition), then "after two years, unable to engage in any occupation for which reasonably fitted by education, training, or experience." This provides, in effect, a two-year period for the insured to be retrained for a different occupation, if possible.

	YOU	SPOUSE
Definition in your policy (1, 2, 3, or 4)	_____	_____

Accident-Only Coverage is a policy that provides coverage only for a disability caused by an accident, not sickness. These policies are less expensive, since accidents are usually less of a threat than sickness. It's best to avoid these policies because they still leave you without coverage for disabilities due to illness.

Insurance Reductions is a provision, included in some group policies, that reduces benefits if disability income is paid from other sources. The purpose is to avoid supplying a total income that is greater than the income prior to the disability. Group disability income is usually coordinated with workers' compensation, Social Security, and some state temporary disability programs. Individual disability policies may also provide for such reductions.

Social Security

The Social Security System does provide disability benefits to those employees who are covered and who qualify for them. The difficulty, for planning purposes, is that the Social Security law provides for the strictest definition of disability—the "any occupation" definition—and requires that the disability be permanent or expected to last at least one year. In 1983, for example, Social Security initially turned down 66 percent of the applications for disability benefits. For this reason, it's unwise to depend only on receiving disability income from Social Security. When payable, Social Security benefits don't begin until five months have elapsed from the beginning of the disability.

Evaluation of Disability Coverage

Review your disability coverage as described above and ask yourself the following questions: Do you have long-term disability coverage? If you do, is there a gap between the ending of your short-term coverage and the commencement of your long-term coverage? (Example: short-term coverage lasts for two months and long-term coverage has a waiting period of six months; this leaves a four-month gap.) Will your long-term coverage provide benefits until you are sixty-five? Are the benefit amounts adequate compared to your after-tax income when working?

Check here whether you think your family's disability income coverage is:

	YOU	SPOUSE
Adequate	_____	_____
Possibly inadequate	_____	_____
Definitely inadequate	_____	_____

Medical Care Insurance

There's nothing like today's medical bills to blow a hole in your budget or even wipe out all your assets—if you don't have insurance. Most workers are covered by group health insurance at their workplace. These group plans vary greatly, from the bare-bones variety to those that are super-deluxe. If you have group coverage, you may not need to buy much, if any, supplementary individual coverage. However, you may still find it worthwhile to complete the rest of this section, especially the part on major medical coverage, to help you understand your coverage better.

If you *don't* have group health coverage, obtaining individual health coverage should be near the top of your priority list. Few things can be as devastating financially as a serious illness involving hospitalization.

Check below whether you or your spouse are covered by group health insurance and also exactly who it covers:

Your group health insurance covers:

You_____Your spouse_____Your dependent children_____

Your spouse's group health insurance covers:

Your spouse_____You_____Your dependent children_____

There are two main categories of medical care coverage: basic coverage and major medical coverage. Modern group plans tend to combine them, with emphasis on major medical, while individual plans may treat them separately.

Basic Coverage

Basic coverage provides insurance against specific types of medical care costs. It's usually available from insurance companies or Blue Cross/Blue Shield organizations and covers one or more of the following types of expenses. You may want to write down what your policy provides. If it provides full coverage on any or all of these, simply use a check mark (√):

Hospital Expense insurance is intended to cover a part if not all of the expenses of hospitalization.

	YOU	SPOUSE
Amount per day	$_____	$_____
Maximum number of days	_____	_____
Additional hospital expenses	$_____	$_____
Diagnostic X-ray and lab work	$_____	$_____
Deductible (if any)	$_____	$_____

Surgical Expense coverage is intended to cover at least part of the costs of surgery.

	YOU	SPOUSE
Highest fee on surgical schedule (schedule limit)	$_____	$_____

Regular Medical insurance covers certain doctors' fees other than fees for surgery.

	YOU	SPOUSE
Dollars per day	$_____	$_____
Number of days	_____	_____

Today these basic coverages are frequently combined into a single package product. A combined Blue Cross/Blue Shield product is also available in many areas.

Basic coverage is important. It provides coverage for specific expenses that can be quite serious. However, it also has some weaknesses. The benefit amounts may not be sufficient, or may become insufficient due to inflation, and there may be expenses not covered. One important weakness is that the benefits run out after a certain number of days, so a lengthy hospital stay can be disastrous. In response to these problems a different type of coverage was developed in the 1950s, called "major medical."

Major Medical Coverage

Major medical plans were originally designed to pick up where basic coverage left off. They provided coverage against catastrophic medical expenses, but did not come into play in normal situations. To accomplish this they utilized two concepts: the deductible and coinsurance. The maximum amount payable under major medical may be as high as $1 million. In fact, some plans have no upper limit. Write down whether you have major medical–type coverage and the maximum amount.

	YOU	SPOUSE
Major medical	_____	_____
Maximum	$_____	$_____

The *Deductible* is a key element of major medical. Its function is to keep premium costs lower and more affordable by screening out most small claims. Major medical tends to use high deductibles, such as $250 or even $1,000 per year (or per illness).

	YOU	SPOUSE
Deductible	$_____	$_____

Coinsurance is the concept that the insured person should bear part of the cost so he or she has an incentive to keep the cost as low as possible. Typically, the insurance company pays 80 percent of any expenses after the deductible has been met and the insured person pays 20 percent. This removes most of the burden from the insured person but still provides a financial incentive to keep costs down.

	YOU	SPOUSE
Coinsurance percentage	_____%	_____%

The *stop-loss amount*—a third concept that has recently become important, especially in comprehensive group insurance plans—is the idea that the insured person should never have to pay more than a certain amount each year in medical expenses under the coinsurance provision. A typical stop-loss amount is $1,500 per year. This usually means that the deductible amount plus the coinsurance share (20 percent in the above example) can never exceed $1,500 a year. When it does, the insurer will pick up 100 percent of any additional covered medical costs. This stop-loss amount may be per person or per family.

The significance of this for financial planning is that with a $1,500 stop-loss per family you don't need a contingency reserve of more than $1,500 a year for medical expenses.

	YOU	SPOUSE
Stop-loss amount	$_____	$_____

Cost Containment

Medical insurance has become very expensive in recent years as medical costs have increased at a rate well in excess of the cost of living index. To protect you and your plan from some of these rising costs, your group insurance carrier may have instituted cost-control measures, such as preadmission review of hospitalization, requesting a second doctor's opinion before surgery, and more stringent claim controls.

If you're purchasing individual medical care insurance, you can reduce your premium by requesting a higher deductible and making sure that you don't request more coverage than you need. There's no easy way to save money, because the alternative—not carrying health insurance at all—leaves you vulnerable to financial disaster.

Health Maintenance Organization (HMOs)

A relatively new form of health care delivery system, called the Health Maintenance Organization or HMO, has been gaining in popularity. Instead of operating on a fee-for-service basis, where you wait until you visit the hospital or doctor and then get reimbursed for the amount charged, HMOs operate on a prepaid basis. You pay a certain amount per month in advance and then use the HMO for whatever medical services you need. HMOs have an incentive to try to keep you healthy and out of the hospital rather than just pay your bills after you go in. They frequently emphasize preventive medicine.

The coverage offered by an HMO is often broader than that offered by regular health insurance. The premium may or may not be higher.

One perceived limitation for some people is that you must choose a doctor from the HMO's list of participating physicians. That physician then becomes your own family doctor. The HMO also has arrangements with its own specialists. Be sure to consider the distance from your home to the HMO, and find out the approximate waiting time for appointments.

HMOs are growing rapidly because many people find them to be an efficient and cost effective way of obtaining medical care services. They are frequently available from your employer as an alternative to your normal health coverage. Give them careful consideration if available.

Evaluation of Medical Care Insurance

Check below whether you feel your medical care insurance is:

	YOU	SPOUSE
Adequate	_____	_____
Possibly inadequate	_____	_____
Definitely inadequate	_____	_____

Homeowners/Renters Insurance

Imagine how you'd feel if a fire reduced your home or apartment to ashes or your cherished possessions were hauled off by a burglar. Or consider the nightmare that would occur if a visitor slipped on your front stairs and successfully sued you for $50,000! Homeowners and renters insurance can help protect you against such disasters.

The three main elements of coverage are insurance on your house (i.e., the structure itself), coverage for your personal property, and protection against liability for bodily injury or damage caused to the person or property of others due to your negligence. The standard homeowners policy is a "package deal" containing all three types of coverage. The standard renters or condominium policy offers only the last two (personal property and liability), since the dwelling structure is not covered.

Your Home

If you took a mortgage to purchase your home, you were probably required to obtain homeowners insurance. However, this doesn't guarantee that the amount of insurance was adequate—even at the time you bought it. As the house becomes older, the expense to replace it increases because of rising construction costs and inflation.

To see if your insurance is adequate, fill in the blanks below:

Approximate replacement cost
of your home (see box) $_____

Your dwelling coverage amount
(often called "coverage A") in
your policy $_____

If you don't insure your home for at least 80 percent of its full replacement cost, you will get less than full reimbursement on any structural damage claims submitted.

The Replacement Cost of Your Home

How do you calculate the replacement cost of your house? Don't assume it is equal to the market value of the house (i.e., the value of the house and land minus the value of the land), because this is not necessarily true. Replacement cost refers to the cost of labor and materials to rebuild your house, or any part of it, in today's market. Many insurance companies will provide a free booklet for you to use in estimating the value. Alternatively, your insurance representative should be able to estimate the value for you.

Many companies offer forms of inflation coverage or guaranteed replacement coverage for a small extra premium.

Exclusions

There are certain exclusions that apply to all homeowners policies. The most important of them are:

Business Use. If you conduct any type of business in your house, even giving piano lessons, you may invalidate your homeowners insurance coverage. You may need an endorsement or even separate commercial coverage. Don't fool around with this one—check with your insurance representative.

Flooding. Damage due to flooding and most groundwater hazards is *not* covered by your homeowners policy. If you have any inkling that you may have a problem, you should investigate further. Homeowners in flood-prone areas may be eligible for flood insurance administered by the federal government if certain land-use restrictions are in force in your municipality.

Earthquake. Damage due to earthquakes or earth movement is generally not covered, but coverage may be available in some areas for an extra premium.

Nuclear hazard. Damage due to any nuclear hazard is not usually covered.

Named Peril vs. All Risk

There are two types of homeowners policies. Named peril policies insure only against certain named perils—such as fire, wind damage, and theft—while all risk policies cover all risks except for those specifically excluded, such as flooding, earthquake, and nuclear hazard. In general, the broader the coverage, the higher the premium. The type of coverage is identified by a code beginning with HO, such as HO-1 or HO-2. Write down here the "HO" number on your policy.

HO - _____

HO-1, **Basic Policy,** insures you against loss or damage from eleven named perils. This type represents about 7 percent of all homeowners policies sold.

HO-2, **Broad Form,** insures you against loss or damage from eighteen named perils and represents about 31 percent of all homeowners policies sold.

HO-3, **Special** or **All Risk,** is the broadest possible coverage on the building and covers against all risks except those specifically excluded (such as flooding or earthquake). This type of policy has slightly less coverage on personal property (eighteen named perils), and it represents about 61 percent of all homeowners policies sold. This is the most popular form because it meets the needs of most people.

HO-5, **Comprehensive,** is the broadest possible coverage on both the building and your possessions. It covers against all risks except those specifically excluded. The most expensive type, it represents less than 1 percent of all homeowners policies sold.

Renters Insurance/Condominium Insurance

HO-4, **Renters Policy,** provides coverage for your personal property (not for the building) against the eighteen named perils. Insurance on the building is the responsibility of the landlord.

HO-6, **Condominium Policy,** provides coverage similar to renters policy on your belongings. Insurance on the building is the responsibility of the condominium association.

Personal Property

Personal property is subject to loss or damage from the same perils as the house itself. However, some of the perils, such as theft, are far more pertinent to personal property than to a house!

Under a homeowners policy (HO-1, HO-2, HO-3, and HO-5) you are automatically covered for one-half the basic coverage amount against loss or damage to your personal property. If your home is insured for $100,000, your personal property is automatically insured for $50,000, unless you request a higher amount. For renters or condominium policies (HO-4 and HO-6), you must select the amount of coverage appropriate for your needs. Write the amount you have below:

Personal property coverage $ _____

(50 percent of dwelling coverage amount, or amount selected)

Don't automatically assume that the amount above is adequate. There are important exclusions and limits that you need to know. And, in general, people tend to underestimate the value of their personal property.

> ## Inventory
>
> It is important to take a complete inventory of your personal property. Simply use a pad of paper with a new page for each room, and list every single item of property, together with its original price, current market value, and serial number or identification mark (if any). Some insurance companies make such forms available for your use free of charge. Be sure to include contents of drawers and closets. Taking pictures (or even a videotape!) of major items is an excellent idea. Such an inventory will be invaluable if you suffer a burglary, fire, or other severe damage. Experience shows that most people cannot recall all of their personal property and do not get full value from their insurance coverage when disasters occur. A copy of the inventory should be kept in a safe deposit box or other secure place *outside the house.*

Limits on Personal Property   The most serious problem with personal property insurance is the failure to realize that there are dollar limits on certain types of property for losses caused by theft and other perils. The stolen diamond ring worth $5,000 may get you only $500 from the insurance company—unless you purchase a special endorsement or rider covering it. In the following chart, write the value of your personal property in the appropriate categories and the amount your policy would pay if the items were stolen.

	COL. 1 VALUE	COL. 2 YOUR POLICY LIMIT	COL. 3 (USUAL POLICY LIMIT)
Cash	$_____	$_____	($100)
Financial documents (stocks, bonds, etc.)	_____	_____	($500)
Boats	_____	_____	($500)
Jewelry and Furs	_____	_____	($500)
Silverware and Gold	_____	_____	($1,000)
Guns	_____	_____	($1,000)
Cameras	_____	_____	
Musical instruments	_____	_____	
Fine arts	_____	_____	
Other	_____	_____	

The amounts listed in columns 2 and 3 are *totals* per occurrence, not amounts per item. For all the jewelry and furs you lose in one burglary, you will receive a total of only $500. Some companies have recently doubled some of these amounts, but they still will not provide sufficient coverage for any item of significant value.

The solution is to either increase the limits on the various kinds of personal items (for an extra premium) or else buy a personal articles "floater" as a separate policy or as an endorsement to your regular policy. The floater insures specific items for their full value and provides coverage wherever the items are located.

Liability Insurance

For financial planning purposes, a very serious risk of loss is your liability as a homeowner or renter for injuries or damage to others. An example is the person who falls on your front steps and sues you for thousands of dollars in damages.

Liability coverage to protect you against this sort of loss is included automatically in your homeowners or renters policy. The limit of liability will often be something like $25,000, which is not necessarily adequate. Check your policy and write down what your liability limit is.

Limit of liability coverage $ _____

The limit can be increased for a small extra premium. You probably want to carry at least $100,000 of liability coverage. If you have any substantial amount of assets to protect, you may also want to consider "personal catastrophe" or "umbrella" coverage (see page 56).

Most policies include a provision for payment of small medical bills, typically up to $1,000, if someone is hurt on your property. This doesn't cover injuries to you or your family.

Policies in most states do *not* cover Workers Compensation—when, for example, a housecleaner falls and is hurt while working for you. If you have any such employees, see your insurance representative for advice. It may be possible to cover this situation by endorsement, or you may need a separate policy.

Evaluation of Your Homeowners/Renters Coverage

Adequate   _____

Possibly inadequate   _____

Definitely inadequate   _____

Automobile Insurance

When it comes to driving, you should give special thought to protection for damage done to the person or property of others. The awesome destruction unleashed by a ton of metal moving at only 40 miles per hour must be seen to be believed. Additional coverages—such as collision, comprehensive, uninsured motorist, and medical payments—are also important. Many aspects of auto insurance are affected by the no-fault concept enacted in a number of states.

Liability Insurance

If an accident occurs due to your negligence and someone is permanently disabled, you may wind up being sued for millions of dollars in damages. The key liability coverage is bodily injury liability insurance, which protects you from claims resulting from the injury or death of another *person.* The other important coverage is property damage liability, which covers you for claims resulting from damage to the *property* of others.

Most policies express liability coverage in a form such as $50/100/25, which means the insurance company will pay up to $50,000 for bodily injury to one person and up to $100,000 for all injuries in one accident. The third figure, 25, means the company will pay up to $25,000 for property damage caused in an accident. (This is usually damage to the other car.)

If you have any assets to protect, you should have at least $100/300/ 50 coverage, and also consider a "personal catastrophe" or "umbrella" policy to increase your insurance to $1 million or more. (See page 56.)

Some newer policies have a single liability limit, such as $100,000 rather than the $50/100/25 arrangement.

Write down what your present liability coverage is:

———————— / ———————— / ————————

Collision

Collision insurance pays for damage to your car caused by collision with another vehicle or some stationary object. It pays regardless of who's at fault for the accident. (If it's the other driver's fault, your company will pay immediately under the collision coverage and then pursue the claim with the other driver.)

Collision insurance normally has a deductible amount, often $100 or more. One of the best ways to reduce your premium is to take a higher deductible—perhaps even $500 or $1,000. You risk losing the amount of the deductible if your car is damaged, but the premium savings are substantial. Ask your insurance representative for premium quotes with different deductibles.

If your car is older, you may well be better off with no collision coverage at all. Simply compare the book value of your car with the premium charged.

Write down whether or not you have collision insurance (yes or no) and the deductible amount:

Yes————   No————   Deductible $————

Comprehensive

Comprehensive coverage, as the name implies, covers almost any kind of damage to your car other than that covered by collision insurance. Fire, theft, and vandalism are several risks covered. Comprehensive, like collision, usually has a deductible amount.

Write down whether you have comprehensive coverage and the deductible amount.

Yes _____   No _____   Deductible $ _____

Uninsured Motorists Coverage

If you or passengers in your car are hurt in an accident caused by another driver, and that driver does not have liability insurance, you may find it very difficult to collect. In this situation, uninsured motorists coverage will protect you from loss up to its coverage limit. However, in order to collect on a claim, it is necessary to show that the other driver was at fault. This coverage is inexpensive and the limit should be the same as for your liability coverage. A variation of this protects against underinsured motorists—where the other driver is at fault and has some insurance but not enough to pay for all of your losses.

Check here if you have

Uninsured motorists coverage	Yes _____	No _____
	Limit $ _____	
Underinsured motorists coverage	Yes _____	No _____
	Limit $ _____	

Medical Payments Coverage

Medical payments insurance covers injuries to you, and any passengers in your car, regardless of which driver was at fault. You don't have to sue the other driver, even if he or she was at fault. You choose the limits, which are typically fairly small, such as $10,000 per person. In no-fault states, this may be replaced by personal injury protection (see next page).

Check below if you have medical payments coverage and the amount:

Medical payments coverage	Yes _____	No _____
	Amount $ _____	

No-Fault Insurance

No-fault insurance is an interesting concept that has been implemented in a number of states. The no-fault systems vary considerably from state to state.

The theory is simple and straightforward. Previously, auto victims had to sue the other driver and prove fault in order to collect for injuries. In many cases, fault could not be proven and the victim was left without reimbursement for hospital and medical bills. Even if fault was proven, the reimbursement did not come until after the lawsuit had been settled, and delays of several years were common.

The idea of pure no-fault was to eliminate lawsuits and have victims simply reimbursed by their own insurance companies for their medical expenses, without any reimbursement for "pain and suffering." This would eliminate the "fault" concept and allow immediate reimbursement for bodily injuries. However, no state has enacted such a pure version of no-fault. All allow lawsuits if there are severe injuries, prolonged disability, or expenses accumulated above a certain threshold.

In practical terms, no-fault means you have something called "personal injury protection" as part of your policy. The personal injury protection (P.I.P.) allows you to determine in advance how much protection you want in case of an accident. You have a certain amount of coverage for medical expenses, and possibly a certain amount for other expenses, such as loss of income. These provisions vary from state to state and there may be additional ones. If your state has no-fault insurance, write down what your policy provides in each instance:

Medical expense $_____

Other coverage $_____

Most states with no-fault insurance require you to carry both liability coverage and personal injury protection.

Evaluation of Coverage

Check below whether you feel your automobile coverage is:

Adequate   _____

Possibly inadequate   _____

Definitely inadequate   _____

"Personal Catastrophe" or "Umbrella" Liability Coverage

Even if you have both homeowners/renters insurance and automobile insurance, you may need additional liability coverage to protect you against a truly large loss. As mentioned earlier, lawsuits seeking damage awards of a million dollars or more are becoming more common, and such a damage award could wipe out all your assets if not covered by insurance.

To provide peace of mind against the risk of such large losses, insurance companies have developed special policies that will cover you against losses that exceed your auto or homeowners limits. They are usually called "umbrella" or "personal catastrophe" policies. A typical policy provides $1 million of coverage. It requires underlying auto liability coverage of $100/300/50 and underlying homeowners liability coverage of $100,000. In addition to covering excess liability of auto or homeowners coverage, it may cover other types of liability for personal injury or property damage that are not covered by either of these. However, it does not provide coverage for any business-related activities. The premium is relatively inexpensive—perhaps $100 a year for a million dollars of coverage.

Write down whether you have personal catastrophe or umbrella coverage and the maximum liability amount.

Yes_____   No_____   Amount $_____

Check whether you feel your protection against such a loss is:

Adequate   _____

Possibly inadequate   _____

Definitely inadequate   _____

Insurance Checklist

For convenience, transfer the evaluations of your various types of insurance to this single sheet for use in chapter nine ("Implementation").

	ADEQUATE	POSSIBLY INADEQUATE	DEFINITELY INADEQUATE
Life insurance (p. 35)			
You	_____	_____	_____
Spouse	_____	_____	_____
Disability income insurance (p. 42)			
You	_____	_____	_____
Spouse	_____	_____	_____
Medical care insurance (p. 45)			
You	_____	_____	_____
Spouse	_____	_____	_____
Homeowners/renters insurance (p. 48)	_____	_____	_____
Automobile insurance (p. 52)	_____	_____	_____
Personal catastrophe insurance (p. 56)	_____	_____	_____

Chapter Six

Investments

An Investment Strategy: Where Should You Put Your Money?

In the last couple of decades, the financial world has changed dramatically for individual investors. Interest rates go up and down in unpredictable fashion. Inflation has become a part of our lives, and new financial instruments have become popular.

Of course, all of these changes have provided average individuals with more opportunities to make money on their money. But with these opportunities come risks. You need to decide which investments are right for you.

No single book or guide could possibly give you all the information you need to make these decisions accurately. Much reading, studying, and a certain amount of luck are required to avoid errors. Competent investment advice can be very useful. However, there are some basic principles to follow.

Obviously, everyone has the same basic goal in mind: to make as much money as possible, after taxes and expenses. But that's not such a simple concept. There is no one right investment for everyone. You need to think about your own personal goals (see chapter two): Do you plan to use the money you invest as an emergency fund, for education or retirement, or for some other purpose? You also need to think about your own tax situation (see chapter four): Do you want current income or long-term capital gains? Do other tax strategies, such as deferral, make sense for you?

In addition, there are three major ideas to keep in mind when investing: liquidity, risk, and return. Any investment you consider should be evaluated on the basis of these three concepts. (Another factor—diversification—is discussed later.)

Return on an investment refers to the money you make on it (or, conceivably, the money you lose on it). The return may take the form of income—such as interest, dividends, or rent—or it may take the form of capital gains or losses.

Liquidity means your ability to get your money out of an investment quickly and with minimum loss if you need it. If you think the cash you are investing might be needed on very short notice, you should only consider investments with a high degree of liquidity. If you believe you won't need the money on short notice, then you can consider investments with less liquidity. Other things being equal, the less liquidity an investment has, the more return you should expect from it.

Risk represents the possibility that the actual return from an investment might differ from the expected return. Some investments, like Treasury bills, have virtually no risk; the federal government stands behind them. Others, like stocks, vary depending on the company and market conditions. As a general rule, the higher the risk involved, the greater the potential return.

Inflation and Compound Interest

Inflation deprives you of the purchasing power of your money: It raises the price of things you want to buy, in effect decreasing the value of each dollar.

But there's a flip side to that coin. Shrewd investing can allow your money to grow even more rapidly than inflation can eat into its value. If, for example, inflation runs at a compound rate of 6 percent over the next ten years, and you have your money in investments providing an after-tax return of the same amount, you'll come out just about even. If you invest them in instruments with a better after-tax return, you'll gain in purchasing power.

The table on page 60 shows, over the course of twenty years, the effect of different interest rates on $10. So, if you put $10 in an investment that earns 8 percent compound interest, you have $46.61 after twenty years.

The table also shows the bad news about inflation. If the inflation rate runs at only 5 percent, something that costs you $10 today will cost you $26.53 in twenty years.

Thinking About Investing

Every time you decide to make an investment, you must consider exactly where you want to put your money. There is no such thing as a single investment that can be used for every occasion or need. For example, if you are sixty years old and putting money away toward retirement, you may want to avoid any major risks. If you are thirty and you're saving toward retirement, then you may be willing to take somewhat bigger chances.

INTEREST RATE

YEAR	5%	8%	10%	12%	15%
0	10.00	10.00	10.00	10.00	10.00
1	10.50	10.80	11.00	11.20	11.50
2	11.03	11.66	12.10	12.54	13.23
3	11.58	12.60	13.31	14.05	15.20
4	12.16	13.60	14.64	15.73	17.49
5	12.76	14.69	16.11	17.62	20.11
6	13.40	15.86	17.72	19.74	23.13
7	14.07	17.14	19.49	22.11	26.60
8	14.77	18.51	21.44	24.76	30.59
9	15.51	19.99	23.58	27.73	35.18
10	16.29	21.59	25.94	31.06	40.46
11	17.10	23.32	28.53	34.79	46.52
12	17.96	25.18	31.38	38.96	53.50
13	18.86	27.20	34.52	43.63	61.53
14	19.80	29.37	37.97	48.87	70.76
15	20.79	31.72	41.77	54.74	81.37
16	21.83	34.26	45.95	61.30	93.57
17	22.92	37.00	50.54	68.66	107.61
18	24.07	39.96	55.60	76.90	123.75
19	25.27	43.16	61.16	86.13	142.32
20	26.53	46.61	67.28	96.46	163.67

When evaluating risk and return, you should always look at the risk and return of your entire portfolio, not just the risk and return of an individual investment. *Diversification* can be very important. Every investment has some risk. Even government-insured bank accounts may be vulnerable (to the risk of inflation). But through diversification it may be possible to combine a variety of investments so that the risk of the overall portfolio is reduced.

One of the most useful concepts in thinking about your investment strategy is called an "investment pyramid." The diagram on page 61 shows approximately how a number of investments relate to one another in terms of risk and return.

Generally speaking, the higher up on the pyramid you find an investment option, the riskier it is and the greater your potential for gain. Conversely, the investments that appear closer to the base of the pyra-

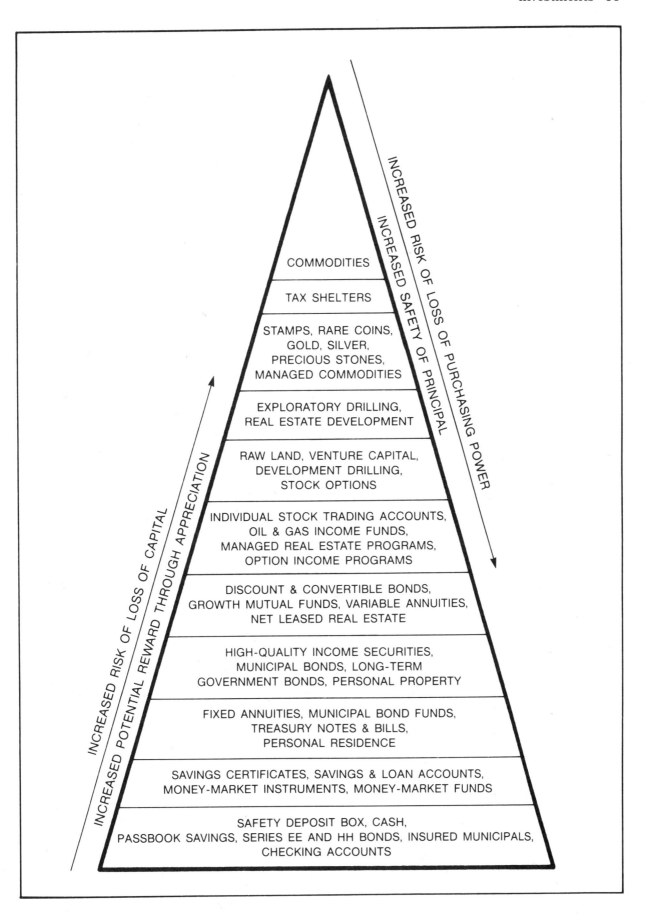

INCREASED RISK OF LOSS OF PURCHASING POWER

INCREASED SAFETY OF PRINCIPAL

INCREASED RISK OF LOSS OF CAPITAL

INCREASED POTENTIAL REWARD THROUGH APPRECIATION

COMMODITIES

TAX SHELTERS

STAMPS, RARE COINS,
GOLD, SILVER,
PRECIOUS STONES,
MANAGED COMMODITIES

EXPLORATORY DRILLING,
REAL ESTATE DEVELOPMENT

RAW LAND, VENTURE CAPITAL,
DEVELOPMENT DRILLING,
STOCK OPTIONS

INDIVIDUAL STOCK TRADING ACCOUNTS,
OIL & GAS INCOME FUNDS,
MANAGED REAL ESTATE PROGRAMS,
OPTION INCOME PROGRAMS

DISCOUNT & CONVERTIBLE BONDS,
GROWTH MUTUAL FUNDS, VARIABLE ANNUITIES,
NET LEASED REAL ESTATE

HIGH-QUALITY INCOME SECURITIES,
MUNICIPAL BONDS, LONG-TERM
GOVERNMENT BONDS, PERSONAL PROPERTY

FIXED ANNUITIES, MUNICIPAL BOND FUNDS,
TREASURY NOTES & BILLS,
PERSONAL RESIDENCE

SAVINGS CERTIFICATES, SAVINGS & LOAN ACCOUNTS,
MONEY-MARKET INSTRUMENTS, MONEY-MARKET FUNDS

SAFETY DEPOSIT BOX, CASH,
PASSBOOK SAVINGS, SERIES EE AND HH BONDS, INSURED MUNICIPALS,
CHECKING ACCOUNTS

mid are somewhat safer, but usually provide less return, and as such mean you may run yet another kind of risk: that of losing purchasing power over time.

Here are some questions that you should ask yourself when you are considering various investment options:

Q. Is my job secure?

If you have a guaranteed, secure stream of income that will certainly cover all your basic expenses, then you can more easily take risks with your money. But if there is a possibility that this cash may be needed as an emergency fund, don't fool around—pick a solid, secure, liquid place to put the money.

Q. Is this investment aimed at a specific, important expense (for example, retirement or college education)?

There's nothing wrong with taking some risks on money you are aiming at specific projects. But be wary of deals with high odds. Speculative investments should be made with money you will not necessarily need. It's not going to be easy to explain to your eighteen-year-old that she can't go to college because the price of precious rubies went down last year.

Q. Am I making this money work as hard for me as it can?

Most of the financial advice you hear is cautionary—don't do this, don't do that. But there are two sides to an investment decision: risk and reward. Don't be frightened out of taking *any* risk—that can be just as foolish as taking too great a risk. Remember that more risk generally means the possibility of greater reward.

Q. Might I be better off repaying debt with this money?

If you have lots of outstanding debt on which you are paying interest, your best investment might be retiring the debt. While the calculations can get a little complicated, especially if you factor in tax implications, the underlying reasoning is simple. If you are paying 18 percent a year on some long-standing credit card debts, then it clearly doesn't pay to invest your money in bonds that will bring in 9 percent a year.

Q. Do I really understand the investment I'm considering?

There are only a few hard and fast rules in this book. One of them is: Never invest in something you don't understand. Ultimately, you may want to make your investments on the advice of someone else—a broker, for example—and that's fine. But it's your money and you should know where it's going. If you come out ahead that way, you'll be able to feel pride in yourself. If you come out behind, there will be no hard feelings or recriminations. Even financial advisers for the wealthiest individuals insist on those individuals understanding their investments.

Your Investment Options

Up until this point we've been speaking of investments in the most general terms. But when it comes time to actually place your hard-earned money on the line, you can't simply ask for an investment that offers, say, no risk, lots of liquidity, and enormous return. You've got to make your way through the numerous investment opportunities available, select a few that are worth pursuing, educate yourself about them, and ultimately make your investment.

On pages 64–70 is a list of commonly available investments with short explanations of each. Of course, the list is not all-inclusive. New kinds of financial instruments are continually being developed. There are even products from other financial areas that have some investment characteristics, such as variable or universal life insurance policies. But this list covers most of the basic alternatives for the purpose of devising an overall investment strategy.

Of course, with any investment decision, the tax consequences can be very important. So, a broad outline of the tax treatment of each of the investments is included. For a more detailed discussion of some of these tax concepts, see chapter four.

As you read the descriptions, consider whether you have the particular investments already, or whether you should investigate any of them further. If you have already put money into some of these investments, it's also useful to consider whether the amount you have invested is right for you, based on your savings goals.

At the end of this chapter is an Investment Checklist to help you assemble this information in one neat place.

The Mutual Fund Concept

Several types of investments are available in the form of mutual funds, which can be especially useful for those investors with smaller amounts to invest. Mutual funds offer such investors the chance for diversification of their portfolio as well as professional management.

Say, for example, you'd like to put money into growth stocks, but you only have enough money for a few dozen shares of any major firm and you don't really know which company is the right one. With a mutual fund, you could put your money into a broad portfolio of growth stocks. The fund managers will take over the job of deciding which are the best ones for that particular fund.

Or, say you'd like a steady, tax-free income stream from municipal bonds. But you're nervous about the risk that might be associated with any individual municipality. A municipal bond fund might put your money into a variety of city and state securities.

For the small investor, mutual funds or mutual fund–type products (such as some deferred annuities) are often the best way to invest. Be sure to read the required prospectus carefully and understand any charges or fees before investing in a mutual fund.

A Closer Look at Some Investment Alternatives

The first six types of investments provide safety and stability for your portfolio. Their common characteristic is that your principal is protected.

Savings Accounts. Generally, these accounts are insured by the federal government for up to $100,000 per investor per institution. You and your spouse can be insured for up to $300,000 in a single bank by opening three accounts: one in your name, one in your spouse's name, and one joint account. The safety and liquidity are great, but the interest rates on these accounts are generally about the lowest available.

Tax treatment: You'll pay ordinary income tax on the interest you collect.

Certificates of Deposit. Available through banks or Savings & Loans, these investments (often called "CDs") are also generally insured in the same way as savings accounts. However, you are usually tied into such investments for a set period of time, and you'll pay a penalty if you withdraw the money early. In exchange, the interest rates available are somewhat higher than those on savings accounts.

Tax treatment: You'll pay ordinary income tax on the interest you collect.

Series EE and HH Bonds. These U.S. Savings Bonds are backed by the U.S. government and are very safe. A variable rate feature (for bonds held five years or more) coupled with a fixed rate guarantee (currently 7.5 percent if held to maturity) offer certain advantages, especially for long-term savings.

Tax treatment: The interest on both is free from state and local taxes. Since the EE bonds pay out only when they are redeemed, you won't have to pay any federal income tax on the interest until that time. You'll then pay ordinary income tax. HH bonds pay out semiannually and you'll pay ordinary income taxes on your interest.

Treasury Bills, Notes, and Bonds. The real advantage to these government-backed investments is their safety and the fact that they can be easily sold. However, in exchange for such benefits you will be getting relatively low interest rates. In the case of notes and bonds, you will get regular payments of your interest. Bills, on the other hand, are sold at a discount to their redemption value and no actual cash payments are made; your profit comes by selling the instrument as it reaches or approaches maturity.

Treasury bills have a maturity of from three to six months and a minimum face amount that is generally $10,000. Treasury notes have a maturity between one and five years and a minimum face amount of $1,000. Treasury bonds have a maturity of over five years and a minimum face amount of $1,000.

Tax treatment: All three instruments are free from state and local taxes. All are subject to federal income taxes on interest at ordinary tax rates.

Money Market Funds. These are mutual funds that invest primarily in government securities and bank certificates of deposit. As such, they are relatively safe investments, although they are not usually guaranteed. Since these funds are managed by professionals, you pay about half a percent of your investment to the fund managers. The interest rates offered vary over time, since these funds are usually invested in short-term instruments.

Tax treatment: Varies depending on the nature of the fund. Can provide some tax savings opportunities.

Fixed Rate Annuities. These contracts are designed to accumulate money in order to provide retirement income beginning on the so-called maturity date of the annuity—for example, at age sixty-five. Generally, that income will continue for the rest of your life, though you may also elect to take out your entire investment in one lump sum at a certain point in time. To fund these annuities, you either pay regular premiums over the years (for a retirement annuity) or you pay in one lump sum (for a single premium deferred annuity).

Annuities provide a good form of fixed savings. In addition, they are relatively safe investments that are almost unique in the lifetime payout provision they offer.

As always, you must be very careful about whom you purchase your annuity from. Select a large, highly rated firm, as opposed to an operation that might not be around when it's time for you to collect.

Tax treatment: These investments may offer a tax deferral feature (see chapter four).

Your own home is in a category by itself as an investment option.

Personal Residence. All things considered, you're probably best off considering your house a place to live first, and an investment second. However, over the course of years, housing prices have done very well in many areas, and there are certain tax advantages (see chapter four).

The next seven types of investments are bonds. They are best thought of as a way to "lock in" current interest rates. They provide a different kind of stability—that of a fixed amount of income—but the principal amount is not guaranteed unless the bonds are held to maturity.

Corporate Bonds. These vary in safety from company to company. With a corporate bond you are, in effect, loaning money to a company. It will pay you regular interest payments over time—generally semiannually—and then at the end of a specified period it will return your original investment. Many people invest in corporate bonds specifically to lock into this steady income stream.

You can, however, try to sell your bond at any time before it reaches maturity. There may be some risk involved here. If the interest rates available in the marketplace are higher than when you bought your bond, you will probably get less than the amount you paid for it. If the available interest rates are lower than when you bought it, you will most likely make a profit when you sell.

For example, let's say you bought a newly issued thirty-year bond with a face value of $10,000 and an interest rate of 10 percent. Each of those thirty years you would get $1,000 in interest and at the end of the thirty years you would get your $10,000 back. If you wanted to sell the bond in the meantime, and interest rates had climbed, you would get something less than the $10,000 face value of the bond. If rates had fallen, you'd get more.

Beyond interest rate fluctuations, there is one other risk to corporate bonds: The company may not be able to pay you the money it owes you over time. However, you can protect yourself against such a risk by carefully evaluating the bonds before you purchase them. Two rating services, Standard & Poors and Moody's, rate the safety of most companies' bonds. Check out these ratings before you commit yourself.

Tax treatment: You'll pay ordinary income taxes on the interest from the bonds. Any profit you make if you sell or redeem the bond may be eligible for capital gains treatment.

Convertible Bonds. These are corporate bonds that offer an extra bonus in addition to a regular interest payment: You can trade them in for a set number of shares of the company's common stock. This allows you the possibility of benefiting from an increase in the value of the company's stock.

These may seem like attractive investments, but remember this: You are sacrificing some return on the bond in exchange for this extra feature. So, if the stock price declines, or never goes up enough to make the conversion profitable, you will have come out behind.

Tax treatment: You'll pay ordinary income taxes on the interest from the bonds, and may qualify for capital gains treatment if you sell the bond (or the equity) at a profit.

Zero Coupon Bonds. These increasingly popular instruments work just like other bonds in many ways, but with one crucial difference: With a zero coupon bond your interest payments are reinvested for you —at a rate of interest that is guaranteed to be the same as the zero coupon bond you bought.

As a result, when the bond matures, you receive all your return, as well as the principal, in one lump sum. That means that the amount you will actually pay for a zero coupon bond will generally be substantially less than the amount you will receive when it matures.

Tax treatment: Unfortunately, although you will not receive any of your interest payments on zero coupon bonds, Uncle Sam will tax you as though you have. As a result, zero coupon bonds are not usually worthwhile investments for individuals unless they are put into some kind of tax sheltered arrangement, like an IRA.

Corporate Bond Funds. If you want professional management and diversity of your portfolio, you may want to put your money in a mutual fund made up of corporate bonds.

Tax treatment: You'll pay ordinary income taxes on the interest, and may qualify for capital gains treatment on any profit on shares in the fund.

Municipal Bonds. These are debt obligations of states, municipalities, and other government institutions. They tend to be very safe, since it is unlikely that a state or a city will default on its debts. However, they are not absolutely safe. In the last few years, some governmental entities have come close to default.

Beyond that, these bonds are subject to the same interest rate risks as are corporate bonds (see above). Of course, before investing in any municipal bond, you should check its rating (available from Standard & Poors or Moody's).

Tax treatment: Municipal bonds are exempt from federal income taxes and sometimes from state and local taxes as well. As a result, they make the most sense for investors in higher tax brackets for whom the tax savings offset the fact that their return is generally lower than that on equivalent corporate bonds.

You may qualify for capital gains treatment if you sell or redeem the bonds at a profit.

Municipal Bond Funds. A fund of municipal bonds is generally somewhat safer than any individual municipal bond—you have the advantage of a diverse portfolio that, presumably, will not allow any single investment to become disproportionately important.

Tax treatment: Generally the same as for municipal bonds, but these funds are not usually exempt from state and local taxes unless the fund is designed for that purpose.

Insured Municipal Bonds. These bonds represent loans to city and state governments that have been guaranteed by an insurance company. They are considered very safe, but pay slightly less than equivalent uninsured bonds.

Tax treatment: Same as for municipal bonds.

The next three financial alternatives are equity investments, which means they involve common stocks. Stocks can offer significant opportunities for growth and protection against inflation but without guarantees on either income or principal.

Common Stocks. People usually invest in the stock market for one of two reasons or for a combination of the two: growth from an increase in the stock's price or income from dividends. Many times there is a trade-off between the two types of investment return. If a company is paying out a large percentage of its profits in dividends, then there may be little growth and appreciation of the stock price. On the other hand, if the dividend is small or nonexistent, you are counting on the fact that the company will be reinvesting its money and growing.

Tax treatment: You'll pay ordinary income tax on any dividends you get from your stock. But if you hold onto the stock for a sufficient length of time (see chapter four), the increase in its value may qualify for capital gains treatment.

Equity Mutual Funds. Mutual funds offer diversification and professional management in selecting a portfolio of common stocks. The funds invest in stocks for income or growth or some combination of the two. When selecting an equity mutual fund you should pay close attention to its past track record.

Tax treatment: You'll pay ordinary income taxes on any income that the fund generates, but sale of shares in the fund may qualify for capital gains treatment.

Variable Annuities. During the accumulation period, these operate much like a mutual fund. The main advantage over a mutual fund is the tax deferral feature, but this also presents certain restrictions.

There's another extra offered by many insurance companies today: annuities with flexible investment plans. That is, at your discretion you can choose to have the money in your annuity allocated to any one of a number of investment funds, such as a stock fund, bond fund, or money market fund.

Tax treatment: see chapter four.

Real estate for investment purposes is one of the least liquid investments, but it is considered an excellent inflation hedge.

Real Estate. If you are investing money that you might need suddenly, a direct investment in real estate is probably not a good idea. Land, commercial real estate, or housing (including a second home) can take a long time to convert into cash, as anyone who has ever tried to sell a house knows. However, for a long-term investment, real estate may be an excellent choice.

One good piece of advice you'll get from anyone who has made money in real estate: Know the property. Schemes involving land thousands of miles away from your home often turn into disasters. A prime vacation spot can sometimes turn out to be a swamp. Make sure you actually see the property and know what you're getting.

Tax treatment: Since there are many ways for you to invest in real estate, there are a variety of tax treatments available. Investing in commercial real estate, for example, may give you all sorts of tax benefits from the depreciation on the property. Consult your tax specialist for details on specific investments.

The remaining investments are more speculative, but they may be suitable for some portion of your portfolio. Some can be very risky or almost risk-free, depending on how they are used. You may need expert advice in this area.

Stock Options. Options are increasingly popular instruments that allow you to buy a certain stock at a certain price within a certain span of time (you have an "option" to do so). So, for example, you might have an option to buy a share of ABC company at $10 a share within twelve months. If the option costs you $2, and the company stock rises to more than $12, you can exercise that option at a profit.

Obviously, with stock options there is the possibility of losing your entire investment. In the example above, if the company stock never gets above $12, you won't make a profit if you exercise your option, and some portion or all of your money will be down the drain.

The simple ownership of a stock option is usually a highly risky investment that can have a very high return. Some companies issue stock options to their executives on favorable terms that have the potential to be very profitable.

Tax treatment: Usually you'll pay ordinary income tax on the profits since options are mostly short-term instruments.

Venture Capital. So, you have a brother-in-law who has invented the better mousetrap and wants you to put in a few thousand dollars. Think twice. New business ventures are notoriously risky. Of course, there's a real opportunity to make lots of money if the business takes off, but there's also a chance to lose all you've invested.

In any case, make sure that any venture capital arrangements you make are carefully spelled out on paper. Don't trust handshakes or kitchen-table agreements. All too often they're worth the paper they're not written on.

Tax treatment: Consult your tax specialist. These deals can be structured in any number of ways with various tax consequences.

Collectibles (Stamps, Coins, Medallions). Buy these things if you enjoy collecting them. Then, if they turn out to be a good investment, you'll have an extra bonus. But for a layperson to get involved in such collections as an investment is very risky—only professionals and people willing to devote lots of time to such collections make money.

Tax treatment: Since these investments are generally long-term, they usually qualify for capital gains treatment.

Precious Stones. It's very difficult to make money in precious stones. As with collectibles, you can buy them if you enjoy owning them, but don't count on making money. The markets give an enormous advantage to the professional investor over the layperson.

Tax treatment: Since these investments are generally long-term, they usually qualify for capital gains taxes.

Precious Metals (Gold, Silver, etc.). While a number of people have made lots of money in precious metals over the last few years, these are highly risky investments. You tend to pay fairly large fees for the privilege of buying gold and silver, and it can be nearly impossible to predict the movement of value in such items.

It is true, however, that such precious metals can serve as a good inflation hedge—over a long period of time, the price of gold will generally keep pace with inflation, but that time span can be very, very long.

Tax treatment: If these investments are made for a sufficiently long period, they will qualify for capital gains treatment.

Commodities. With commodities you have the opportunity to make vast sums of money through the use of leverage. You also have the chance to lose all your money. Professional commodity traders understand that you may lose money on most of your investments, and make a lot of money on a few. They have the capital available to take the losses while waiting for the profits. If you don't, you'd best stay clear of commodities.

One additional warning: With many commodity deals you will be borrowing a great deal of money to make the investment. You might put up $2,000 to buy $40,000 worth of sugar, for example, As a result, if the price of sugar goes down, even slightly, your entire $2,000 can disappear. If you want to keep the investment, you have to put up more money.

Tax treatment: Since these are generally not long-term investments, you usually pay ordinary income tax.

Investment Checklist

Now that you've had the chance to get a quick glimpse of an array of investments available to you, it's time to think about how your investment portfolio is arranged, and what changes you may want to make.

The following chart lists the investment opportunities covered. Go through them one at a time, referring to the investment definitions when you need to. If you already have some money invested in any of these options, enter the amount on the line provided. Then decide if you think it's an appropriate amount or if you should be considering increasing or decreasing that investment.

If you have no money in a specific investment, decide whether or not it is an appropriate investment for you to investigate further, and check the proper line. When you are finished you should have a shopping list that will tell you which investments you may want to consider or potentially buy.

Investment Checklist	CURRENT INVEST-MENT	TOO MUCH	PROPER	TOO LITTLE	INVESTIGATE FURTHER?	
					YES	NO
Savings accounts	$_____	____	____	____	____	____
Certificates of deposit	_____	____	____	____	____	____
Series EE and HH bonds	_____	____	____	____	____	____
Treasury bills, notes, and bonds	_____	____	____	____	____	____
Money market funds	_____	____	____	____	____	____
Fixed rate annuities	_____	____	____	____	____	____
Personal residence	_____	____	____	____	____	____
Corporate bonds	_____	____	____	____	____	____
Convertible bonds	_____	____	____	____	____	____
Zero coupon bonds	_____	____	____	____	____	____
Corporate bond funds	_____	____	____	____	____	____
Municipal bonds	_____	____	____	____	____	____
Municipal bond funds	_____	____	____	____	____	____
Insured municipal bonds	_____	____	____	____	____	____
Common stocks	_____	____	____	____	____	____
Equity mutual funds	_____	____	____	____	____	____
Variable annuities	_____	____	____	____	____	____
Real estate	_____	____	____	____	____	____
Stock options	_____	____	____	____	____	____

Investment Checklist	CURRENT INVEST-MENT	TOO MUCH	PROPER	TOO LITTLE	INVESTIGATE FURTHER? YES	NO
Venture capital	$_____	___	___	___	___	___
Collectibles	_____	___	___	___	___	___
Precious stones	_____	___	___	___	___	___
Precious metals	_____	___	___	___	___	___
Commodities	_____	___	___	___	___	___
Other	_____	___	___	___	___	___
Other	_____	___	___	___	___	___
Other	_____	___	___	___	___	___

Chapter Seven

Retirement Planning

It's never too soon to start planning for your retirement. Even if you are still in the market for playpens or your first house, you should be making preparations for the day when you won't be holding down a full-time job. And nowadays, the government has made that idea more attractive than ever through Individual Retirement Accounts and other similar arrangements.

Whatever you can save, the most important thing is not to be caught by surprise. Unfortunately, many Americans find retirement planning so baffling that they simply don't do it. Instead of taking action, they fret. According to a study done by the American Council of Life Insurance, two out of three respondents are at least "somewhat" concerned that they will be caught short when it comes time for retirement.

The first step in planning for retirement is to think about what you will need in order to live and, of course, enjoy yourself after you retire. Generally, experts believe that most people planning on retiring at age sixty-five should shoot for a postretirement income equal to about 70 percent of their preretirement income (85 percent for minimum wage earners and 55 percent for high wage earners). To estimate the annual income you will need after retirement, take your current income and multiply it by the appropriate percentage, such as 70 percent (.70). The result is a goal for your annual post-retirement income, expressed in today's dollars.

Current annual income	×	.70 (or other percentage—see above)	=	Goal for annual post-retirement income
$_____				$_____

You might, however, want to aim for an even greater percentage—it depends on the retirement activities you have in mind.

To calculate the amount more exactly, you may want to prepare a retirement budget showing your expenses before and after you retire. This can easily be done using the budget worksheets in chapter eight.

In fact, getting a fix on your retirement budget becomes especially important as you get closer to retirement age. Whether you use the percentage method or the more exact budget method, you will establish a goal for the annual retirement income you need, expressed in today's dollars.

How Much Money Will You Have?

Now that you have set a goal for how much money you may need when it comes time to retire, it's time for the other half of the equation: Where will that money come from? This isn't really as difficult a calculation as you'd think. Basically, your after-retirement income, assuming that you don't continue to hold down some kind of part-time job, will come from three sources: Social Security, pension plans, and investments. As explained later, there are two types of pension plans to consider. You should make estimates of the amount of income you can expect from Social Security and "defined benefit" pension plans (if any), then subtract that total from the amount you need for retirement. That should give you the amount you will need to receive from your investments and from any "defined contribution" pension plans. The final step is to estimate the additional amount you need to save for retirement purposes.

In order to take inflation into account, these estimates make two important assumptions: first, that your pay level will move in step with inflation for the rest of your working life, and second, that your assets, including your investments, will do the same. The purpose of the assumptions is to keep the calculations simple. They allow you to avoid the quagmire of compound interest tables. While the results are only ballpark figures, for retirement planning purposes they are usually more than adequate.

Social Security

The Social Security system was never designed to provide all the money people need after retirement. But it can certainly help get you there. For a rough estimate of what Social Security may provide for you, find the description of your marital and income status in the following material and follow through with the calculations provided.

Single Person

If you have been making the minimum wage throughout your life (about $7,000 in 1984), you can expect your Social Security benefits to equal about **62** percent of your preretirement income that is subject to Social Security taxes.

If you have been an average wage-earner for your working life (about $16,000 in 1984), Social Security will equal about **41** percent of your preretirement income that is subject to Social Security taxes.

If you have been paying the maximum allowable to Social Security for your working life ($37,800 in 1984), your Social Security benefits will equal about **23** percent of your preretirement income that is subject to Social Security taxes.

Obviously, if you have been making substantially more than the maximum taxable income for Social Security, you will only receive whatever the maximum is when you retire. In 1985 that figure is $8,642 a year at age sixty-five. This could be even less than 23 percent of preretirement income.

Note that the more you earn, the less adequate Social Security by itself is.

Married Person with Nonworking Spouse

This description applies in one of two cases: if one spouse has never worked or if one spouse has worked, but not enough to earn Social Security benefits that are more than half of the other's benefits.

If this applies to you, simply find the benefits for the spouse with the higher income using the single person method, and then add another 50 percent (i.e., multiply by 1.5).

Married Person with Working Spouse

If you and your spouse have worked throughout your lives, you can find a rough estimate of your Social Security income by calculating each of your benefits individually, under the section labeled single person, and then simply adding them together. (If either spouse has spent a number of years out of the labor force, the Social Security benefits might be reduced.)

Now, to estimate how much Social Security will pay you in today's dollars, multiply your current pay by the appropriate percentage from the "Single Person" table above. If your income falls between two of these categories, pick a percentage between those provided. For example if you earn $27,000 a year, which is about halfway between $16,000 and $37,800, pick a percentage such as 32 percent, which is about halfway between 41 percent and 23 percent.

	YOU	SPOUSE
Current income (but not more than Social Security maximum, such as $37,800 in 1984)	$_____	$_____
×		
Approximate Percentage	_____%	_____%
Estimated Social Security income	$_____	$_____

Total (your estimated Social Security income plus your spouse's, or 1.5 times the larger of the two estimated incomes, if that produces a higher total income) $_____

Your Pension

The number of private pension plans has more than doubled in the past decade, and today about 60 percent of workers over age twenty-five are covered by pensions.

Since this may be an important source of retirement income for you, it's vital to understand both how it operates and how much you'll be getting from your pension.

There are two basic kinds of pension plans. The first is called a "defined benefit" pension plan. Under this plan, you are told in advance how to figure out the benefit you will get from your pension when you retire. Your employer and plan administrator will determine, over time, how much money will be contributed to the plan, but the formula for determining the payout is fixed.

The second kind is called a "defined contribution" pension plan. With this type, there is no set benefit for employees. Instead, the employer contributes a set amount of money for each employee on a yearly basis. Then, when an individual retires, that money is used to provide retirement benefits. In some instances, the money may be paid out in a lump sum to the retiree who will invest it. In other cases, the plan administrator will pay out the amount in installments or as an annuity.

Yet another important concept to understand about your pension is the idea of vesting. When you are vested in a plan, you are entitled to receive some benefits from it, even if you leave the company. But if you are not yet vested, you would not receive pension benefits were you to quit tomorrow.

Your company should provide you with a summary plan description to help explain your benefits. If you do not get this kind of information automatically, ask for it.

Note below whether you and your spouse are covered under a defined benefit or defined contribution pension plan:

	YOU	SPOUSE
Defined benefit pension plan	_____	_____
Defined contribution pension plan	_____	_____

The rest of this section is concerned with defined benefit plans because they provide a benefit that is fairly easy to calculate. Defined contribution plans are equally important, but the calculation is handled differently. They are covered on pages 79–80.

If you are covered by a defined benefit pension plan, your employer should be able to tell you what percentage of your pay you can expect from your pension plan at normal retirement age. Get that number, and apply it to your current salary. Remember, too, that many pension plans take Social Security benefits into account when they calculate your benefits. So, be sure to find the pension amount you will receive after any adjustment for Social Security benefits has been deducted.

Also, be sure to determine whether the amount is for a single life annuity or whether it is a joint life annuity that will be continued for your spouse if you die first. If you are married, the law requires that you receive a joint life annuity unless you and your spouse agree on a different payment provision. Some people might opt for the single life annuity, for example, because it has a higher monthly payout. This occurs because the benefits are expected to be paid for a shorter time.

Of course, if you are a member of more than one defined benefit pension plan (remember government or military pensions), you may have to make several phone calls in order to make this calculation.

Enter below the amount you expect to receive annually from defined benefit pensions not including any Social Security benefits payable:

	YOU	SPOUSE
Amount from defined benefit pension plan +	$_____	$_____
Amount from second defined benefit pension plan (if applicable)	$_____	$_____
	$_____ (Your total)	+ $_____ (Spouse's total)
		= $_____ (Total for you and your spouse)

Additional Retirement Income Needed

In just a few moments you should know how much money you need to save each year in order to live comfortably after retirement. Just follow the next five steps.

1. Add together the amount of annual income you have estimated as coming from Social Security and defined benefit pension plans.

Social Security +	$_____
Defined benefit pension plans	$_____
Annual income	$_____

2. Now, go back to the first page of this chapter and see how much income you expected to need to retire comfortably.

Retirement needs $_____
—

Annual income (from above) $_____
_____

Additional retirement income needed $_____

3. The figure above represents the annual amount of income you need to obtain from the assets available at retirement time. How much capital will be required to generate this much income depends entirely on the return you get from your assets. So, if you need $10,000 a year from these assets and interest rates are 10 percent, you will need $100,000 of savings from all sources.

The following computation assumes you leave the entire amount at interest, without touching the principal. (Another alternative is the life annuity providing an income for as long as you live, which is discussed later.)

Since interest rates can vary significantly from year to year, you should probably be reasonably conservative in figuring how much investment principal you need in order to generate the needed investment income. The table below makes this calculation even easier for you. Simply look up the rate of return you expect to get on your money, refer to the factor to its right, and multiply your needed investment income by that factor. That will give you the amount of capital you'll need to provide that much income at the assumed interest rate.

Assumed Interest Rate
on Assets Available
at Retirement

_____

FACTOR
6%-----16.6
8%-----12.5
10%-----10.0
12%----- 8.3

_____

Additional retirement
income needed $_____
×
Factor for chosen per-
cent   _____
=
Lump sum needed $_____

For example, suppose you need an additional $10,000 a year and you expect interest rates of 8 percent to be available at the time you retire. Multiply $10,000 times 12.5 to get $125,000 as the lump sum needed.

4. Fortunately, you probably have a head start on reaching that lump sum figure. You may already have a certain amount of net worth (including defined contribution pension plans). First refer back to chapter one to see the worksheet on which you calculated your current net worth. Obviously, you either won't be able to, or won't want to, sell many of the items listed when you retire. For example, you may want to continue to live in your house. And you probably won't want to part with any collections or jewelry. The cash value of any permanent insurance policies may be available to use for retirement income if you no longer have a need for the coverage provided. So, you should simply figure out that portion of your current net worth that will be used to provide retirement income. This portion of your net worth may be largely made up of investments. Don't forget to also include your current account balance in a defined contribution pension plan, IRA, 401-K, profit-sharing, or thrift plan. Then subtract that from the lump sum needed.

The result of this calculation will be the amount of additional savings you'll need at retirement.

Lump sum needed	$_____
−	
Current assets	$_____
Additional savings needed by retirement	$_____

For example, if you need a lump sum of $125,000 and have a $40,000 current account balance in a defined contribution pension plan and $10,000 in an IRA, you would need an additional $75,000 in savings by retirement time.

5. This is the last step. Take the amount of additional savings you'll need at retirement and divide it by the number of years between now and your retirement date. This will give you the amount in today's dollars you should be saving each year toward your retirement.

Additional savings needed for retirement	$_____
÷	
Number of years until retirement	_____
Savings needed for next year	$_____

This annual savings goal can be met in a number of ways, including any payments toward a defined contribution pension plan, profit sharing or thrift plan, an IRA, or a 401-K.

The part not already being saved through other means is the part you will want to use as your retirement savings goal for budgeting purposes in the next chapter. Write that amount here:

Additional Retirement Savings
Needed Next Year
(for budget purposes): $_____

For example, if you need to save an additional $75,000 by retirement, which is ten years away, you would want to save $7,500 per year. If your employer is putting away $3,000 a year in a defined contribution pension plan for you (use last year's figures for simplicity) and you are saving $2,000 a year in an IRA, you would only need to save an additional $2,500 a year ($7,500 − $5,000).

This annual savings goal is only a rough estimate based on a number of assumptions about inflation, your income, and your continued employment until retirement with the same employer. Its accuracy is very much dependent on the interest rate assumption used (6, 8, 10, or 12 percent). It may be useful to do the calculation again with a different rate of interest. Keep in mind that you need to do the entire calculation every few years in order to adjust the annual savings amount for inflation.

The bottom line is this: A financially comfortable retirement is within the reach of most people, but the time to start planning for it is now.

Do You Understand Your Employer's Retirement Plan?

There are a number of questions you may have regarding your pension plan. Do not hesitate to ask your employer about anything you don't understand. The time to straighten out any confusion is while you're still working—not after you retire.

Here are a few questions you might think about asking—if you don't already know the answers.

1. Is your job specifically covered by your company's pension plan? (All pension plans do not cover all employees.)
2. If you retire early, what benefits will you get from the plan?
3. What happens to your group life and group health insurance if you retire early? Can they be continued after your retirement? For how long? Is there an additional cost to you for this coverage?
4. What income will your spouse get from your pension if you should die before retirement?
5. What happens to your group life insurance after you retire at normal retirement age? Is it discontinued or greatly reduced?
6. If you work after you turn sixty-five, will you get additional benefits?

Life Annuity Payout

If you have a large lump sum of money available when you retire, you may find yourself with two contradictory objectives. You want to be able to receive as much income as possible each year, *but* you don't want to run out of money. One solution is the life annuity. A life annuity pays you a monthly income for as long as you live. Even if you live to age 110, you won't outlive your income.

For example, suppose you are age sixty-five with a lump sum of $100,000. You can go to an insurance company and purchase a *straight life annuity* contract for $100,000 that might pay you about $1,160 a month, or about $14,000 a year. The actual amount paid depends on the company's annuity rates at that time. The monthly payment, once established, is guaranteed to you for the rest of your life. When you die, however, the payments stop—even if only a few payments have been received.

Much more popular is the *life annuity, ten years certain*, which provides that at least ten years' worth of payments must be made to you or to your beneficiary, even if you die before the ten years are up. The income is slightly less—$13,000 a year in the example above.

Another common type of life annuity is the *joint and survivor annuity*, which pays an income to you and another person (usually your spouse) for as long as either of you is alive. The income is again less—$11,500 a year in the example above, assuming you and your spouse are both age sixty-five.

The example and the rates described above are for an immediate annuity—where you pay a lump sum and receive the first monthly payment almost immediately. The same type of payout arrangements are available in deferred annuities (after the accumulation period), in pension plans, and in most permanent insurance policies.

How do you decide if an annuity is right for you? Consult your insurance representative, tax adviser, and any other specialist who may be involved. Obtain rate quotations and compare those figures to your alternatives. Consider your health—and that of your spouse if a joint annuity is under consideration. (Life annuities are not a good idea for someone whose health is poor.) Then decide if the unique features of the life annuity are appropriate for your situation.

Some Basic Facts About Medicare

Unhappily, as you grow older, your medical bills are likely to grow bigger. So it's important that you understand exactly what benefits you can expect to receive after retirement both from the government's Medicare program and from any supplemental insurance you have.

To help you get started, here are some basic facts about Medicare to arm you against unpleasant surprises when you're sick and can least afford them.

- The average person can expect Medicare to cover about 40 percent to 50 percent of all medical bills.

- Medicare comes in two parts. As long as you qualify for Social Security, you'll automatically get the hospital insurance (Part A) at no cost. The portion that provides medical insurance outside the hospital (Part B), is optional and costs a moderate amount each month. Most experts believe Part B is well worth getting and that it's a good idea to sign up for it as soon as you qualify.

- You can get Medicare even if you don't retire. (Contact your Social Security office three months before you reach age sixty-five.)

- Not all hospitals accept, or are certified for, Medicare. So always ask about this point before you are treated.

- Medicare does not cover routine physical examinations and tests, eyeglasses, hearing aids, drugs, or any kind of custodial care. (That counts out most nursing homes.)

- Medicare does not generally cover medical expenses incurred while you are out of the country.

- Medicare is not taxable. You don't report the money it contributes to your care on your income tax.

- Medicare has many limitations. Be sure you also consider supplemental insurance coverage to take over where Medicare leaves off.

A Guide to Discounts for Older People

One way you can cut down on your expenses once you retire is by taking advantage of the many discounts and cost-cutting measures available to older people. A sampling:

- Membership in the American Association of Retired Persons. This organization is inexpensive to join and provides free tax assistance, availability of some group insurance benefits, a discount pharmacy service, multiple travel benefits, as well as other money-saving opportunities.

- Travel and entertainment discounts. Hotels, motels, planes, trains, buslines, tours, and restaurants often offer reductions.

- Tax relief. Laws change and vary around the country, but many states do try to make life easier for older people. In some places, for example, you may qualify for a renter's tax credit, a partial property tax exemption, deferred payment options, or other special tax deductions. Check, too, to see if your retirement income is exempted or partially exempted from taxation in your state.

- Drugs. Check for senior citizen discounts, and remember that prescriptions and even over-the-counter drugs are tax deductible. You also may be able to save money by opting for generic drugs instead of name brands.

- Special equipment loans. If you are disabled, even temporarily, and need a wheelchair, walker, or hospital equipment at home, check to see if your local Easter Seal Society is one of the many with a low-cost loan program. Fees are usually set on a sliding scale.

Chapter Eight

Budgeting

The Budgeting Process

Wouldn't it be nice to have enough money to do everything you wanted? Unfortunately, most of us aren't lottery winners or millionaires, and so we have to plan ahead to get what we want.

In previous chapters you thought about your future and the kinds of major goals you would like to set for yourself. Now it's time to sit down and figure out where the money will come from. This is the art of budgeting. You put down your income and your expenses—including your planned savings projects—side by side. Then you work to make the two sets of numbers compatible.

Of course, there is no one method for budgeting that will work for everyone. Some people are comfortable keeping this kind of information on the back of an old envelope—only making detailed budgets on rare occasions. Others prefer more complex record-keeping systems or use home computers to put together an efficient budget. The worksheets in the pages that follow may help you organize your budget. But don't feel that they represent the only method of budgeting. The system you find most useful is best for you.

Whatever method you ultimately choose, the key to mastering your finances is regular monitoring. Working out a lovely budget on January 1 is a great start, but if you don't check every few months (or better yet, every month), to see if you are keeping in line with that budget, your careful work may go for naught.

Naturally, once you have worked out a budget, you may learn that you can't have everything you want with your current income. That doesn't mean you should just shrug your shoulders and give up. Anything you really want is worth working—and waiting—for. You may have to defer some of today's pleasures to reach tomorrow's goals. For example, let's say that you've decided you want a new trailer in four years and will save $2,000 a year toward it. However, when you go through the budgeting process that follows, you discover you're $500 short per year. That's when the choices start. Where are you going to get that $500? You could do something to earn $500 more, or you could start cutting back on current expenses. You might find that restaurants are a big drain on your cash flow. Or trade in sirloin steaks for chopped meat for a while. The choices, as always, are up to you and your family.

As with most financial planning decisions, this budgeting process generally works best when it is a family affair. Unfortunately, getting everyone—including your children—into the same boat can sometimes be a bit tricky. Different ideas and desires have to be taken into account. It won't do for one spouse to decide to give up on expensive meals while the other is buying lobster and truffles. So try to take the time and the energy to talk through your budget with everyone involved. The time spent now may save friction in the future.

Curiously, one of the most important areas to consider in such discussions is one many people ignore: miscellaneous expenses. It's pretty easy to budget the money you're spending on rent or mortgages, and it may not be too hard to figure out how much you should be setting aside for your car, telephone, or utilities, since these are things you generally pay for with a check and as a result have good records of them. But the things you pay for in cash, which can range from restaurant meals to newspapers to toys for your children, can be harder to keep a handle on. Nobody can expect you to keep track of each of these items individually, but it does pay to have some idea of how much you are spending, out of pocket, in a month.

In any case, don't plan on having your budget sheets cast in bronze. Next year, at this time, you should be doing them again.

A Financial Balancing Act

The following worksheets will give you an opportunity to forecast your income for the coming year, to forecast your expenses (including the planned savings for your major goals), and to see if the two work well together. In addition, you'll be able to see the ebb and flow of income and expenses in your household on a monthly basis.

Start off with Worksheet I, which asks for income items. You should be able to get a good start by referring to chapter one for many of these figures. The difference here, of course, is that you'll be entering them on a monthly basis and using take-home income rather than gross income. Many of your income items, such as salary, will be stable from month to month. But others, such as bonuses, dividends, or bond interest, may come only once or twice a year. If you're paid weekly or biweekly, you may want to use four weekly or two biweekly checks as your monthly income, and add the extra paychecks for the months in which they occur. This exercise will help you get a sense of the times of year when you have more or less cash coming into your household. If you have no irregular, seasonal income, you should be able to use only the last two columns of this worksheet.

Next, move on to Worksheet II, which gives you an opportunity to start looking at your expenses. The best place to begin this project is with your expenses for the last twelve months. Using your checkbook register, credit card bills, or records, fill in all the appropriate information for the past year on a monthly basis. The worksheet gives you a head start by providing a number of possible categories of expenses, but you'll also find a number of blank lines for you to fill in. Feel free to re-label lines or double up if necessary (for example, if you have more than three loan payments or more than three life insurance policies). Don't forget to include discretionary items—things like food for the family pet or magazine subscriptions. Remember, too, to include provisions for the expectable but unpredictable, such as car repairs, home repairs, or doctor bills. Also, don't forget seasonal expenses—like holiday presents or summer camps for your children.

In all cases there's no need to make these calculations to the penny. And at all times, use a pencil with an eraser—you'll probably need the eraser.

Then, when you have finished filling in all your monthly expenses for the past year, you can total them up to obtain your yearly expenses, and divide by twelve to find your average monthly expenses. This will give you all the basic information you'll need to move on to Worksheet III. Here you'll use last year's expenses to help you work out a budget for the year to come. Some of the changes may be caused by this book. You may decide to set new savings goals, obtain additional insurance coverage, or increase your credit card payments. Other changes may be a little harder to see. So before you even pick up your pencil to fill out Worksheet III, sit down and think about how your life might be changing in the next twelve months. Is inflation driving food costs up? Will your rent or real estate taxes be increasing? Are there any plans for moves or big trips in the offing?

It might make things somewhat simpler for you, in filling out this worksheet, to start with your estimates of total yearly expenses first. That way, you'll be able to see immediately if your total expenses for next year are out of line with your projected income. After that, you can take the time and trouble to figure out a monthly budget.

As a final step, compare your monthly expenses to your monthly income. Even if your annual income and expenses are balanced, you may find a surplus or deficit for individual months. You may have to save or borrow on a temporary basis to make your cash flow match your expenses.

Budgeting involves a certain amount of effort, but one thing is sure. If you can stick to your plans for the most part, for just one year, the rewards you'll experience come year's end will be enough to make this kind of discipline a habit.

Worksheet I: Income (Year: 19   )

INCOME ITEMS	Jan.	Feb.	March	April	May	June
1. Take-home pay	____	____	____	____	____	____
2. Take-home pay	____	____	____	____	____	____
3. Bonuses	____	____	____	____	____	____
4. Savings Accounts	____	____	____	____	____	____
5. CDs	____	____	____	____	____	____
6. Bonds	____	____	____	____	____	____
7. Annuities	____	____	____	____	____	____
8. Stock dividends	____	____	____	____	____	____
9. Dividends from closely held companies	____	____	____	____	____	____
10. Real estate rental	____	____	____	____	____	____
11. Trust income	____	____	____	____	____	____
12. Child support or alimony	____	____	____	____	____	____
13. Social Security	____	____	____	____	____	____
14. Pension or profit sharing	____	____	____	____	____	____
15. Other _____	____	____	____	____	____	____
16. Other _____	____	____	____	____	____	____
17. Other _____	____	____	____	____	____	____
Total	____	____	____	____	____	____

July	Aug.	Sept.	Oct.	Nov.	Dec.	Total	$\div 12 =$ Average monthly income
————	————	————	————	————	————	————	————————
————	————	————	————	————	————	————	————————
————	————	————	————	————	————	————	————————
————	————	————	————	————	————	————	————————
————	————	————	————	————	————	————	————————
————	————	————	————	————	————	————	————————
————	————	————	————	————	————	————	————————
————	————	————	————	————	————	————	————————
————	————	————	————	————	————	————	————————
————	————	————	————	————	————	————	————————
————	————	————	————	————	————	————	————————
————	————	————	————	————	————	————	————————
————	————	————	————	————	————	————	————————
————	————	————	————	————	————	————	————————
————	————	————	————	————	————	————	————————
————	————	————	————	————	————	————	————————
————	————	————	————	————	————	Total annual income	Average monthly income

Worksheet II: Last Year's Expenses (Year: 19   )

FIXED EXPENSE ITEMS	Jan.	Feb.	March	April	May	June
1. Savings (p. 14)	____	____	____	____	____	____
2. Retirement savings (p. 80)	____	____	____	____	____	____
3. Housing	____	____	____	____	____	____
4. Heat	____	____	____	____	____	____
5. Electricity and gas	____	____	____	____	____	____
6. Telephone	____	____	____	____	____	____
7. Water	____	____	____	____	____	____
8. Property tax	____	____	____	____	____	____
9. Other taxes	____	____	____	____	____	____
10. Life insurance	____	____	____	____	____	____
11. Life insurance	____	____	____	____	____	____
12. Life insurance	____	____	____	____	____	____
13. Health insurance	____	____	____	____	____	____
14. Auto insurance	____	____	____	____	____	____
15. Home insurance	____	____	____	____	____	____
16. Auto loan	____	____	____	____	____	____
17. Loan payment	____	____	____	____	____	____
18. Loan payment	____	____	____	____	____	____
19. Loan payment	____	____	____	____	____	____
20. Transportation (commuting)	____	____	____	____	____	____

Subtotal   ____ ____ ____ ____ ____ ____

July	Aug.	Sept.	Oct.	Nov.	Dec.	Total	$\div 12 =$ Average monthly expenses
____	____	____	____	____	____	____	_____
____	____	____	____	____	____	____	_____
____	____	____	____	____	____	____	_____
____	____	____	____	____	____	____	_____
____	____	____	____	____	____	____	_____
____	____	____	____	____	____	____	_____
____	____	____	____	____	____	____	_____
____	____	____	____	____	____	____	_____
____	____	____	____	____	____	____	_____
____	____	____	____	____	____	____	_____
____	____	____	____	____	____	____	_____
____	____	____	____	____	____	____	_____
____	____	____	____	____	____	____	_____
____	____	____	____	____	____	____	_____
____	____	____	____	____	____	____	_____
____	____	____	____	____	____	____	_____
____	____	____	____	____	____	____	_____

Worksheet II: Last Year's Expenses (Year: 19   ) (Cont'd)

OTHER EXPENSE ITEMS	Jan.	Feb.	March	April	May	June
Subtotal	___	___	___	___	___	___
21. Food	___	___	___	___	___	___
22. Miscellaneous	___	___	___	___	___	___
23. Medical/dental/drugs	___	___	___	___	___	___
24. House repair	___	___	___	___	___	___
25. Clothing	___	___	___	___	___	___
26. Cleaning	___	___	___	___	___	___
27. Current education	___	___	___	___	___	___
28. Auto repair and maintenance	___	___	___	___	___	___
29. Entertainment	___	___	___	___	___	___
30. Gifts	___	___	___	___	___	___
31. Travel	___	___	___	___	___	___
32. Other* ___	___	___	___	___	___	___
___	___	___	___	___	___	___
___	___	___	___	___	___	___
___	___	___	___	___	___	___
___	___	___	___	___	___	___
Total	___	___	___	___	___	___

* Including alimony and child support, pensions, union and professional dues, business expenses, church and charitable expenses, etc.

July	Aug.	Sept.	Oct.	Nov.	Dec.	Total	$\div 12$ = Average monthly expenses
———	———	———	———	———	———	———	———————
———	———	———	———	———	———	———	———————
———	———	———	———	———	———	———	———————
———	———	———	———	———	———	———	———————
———	———	———	———	———	———	———	———————
———	———	———	———	———	———	———	———————
———	———	———	———	———	———	———	———————
———	———	———	———	———	———	———	———————
———	———	———	———	———	———	———	———————
———	———	———	———	———	———	———	———————
———	———	———	———	———	———	———	———————
———	———	———	———	———	———	———	———————
———	———	———	———	———	———	———	———————
———	———	———	———	———	———	———	———————
———	———	———	———	———	———	———	———————
———	———	———	———	———	———	———	———————
———	———	———	———	———	———	Total annual expenses	Total monthly expenses

Worksheet III: Next Year's Estimated Expenses (Year: 19   )

FIXED EXPENSE ITEMS	Jan.	Feb.	March	April	May	June
1. Savings (p. 14)	____	____	____	____	____	____
2. Retirement savings (p. 80)	____	____	____	____	____	____
3. Housing	____	____	____	____	____	____
4. Heat	____	____	____	____	____	____
5. Electricity and gas	____	____	____	____	____	____
6. Telephone	____	____	____	____	____	____
7. Water	____	____	____	____	____	____
8. Property tax	____	____	____	____	____	____
9. Other taxes	____	____	____	____	____	____
10. Life insurance	____	____	____	____	____	____
11. Life insurance	____	____	____	____	____	____
12. Life insurance	____	____	____	____	____	____
13. Health insurance	____	____	____	____	____	____
14. Auto insurance	____	____	____	____	____	____
15. Home insurance	____	____	____	____	____	____
16. Auto loan	____	____	____	____	____	____
17. Loan payment	____	____	____	____	____	____
18. Loan payment	____	____	____	____	____	____
19. Loan payment	____	____	____	____	____	____
20. Transportation (commuting)	____	____	____	____	____	____
Subtotal	____	____	____	____	____	____

July	Aug.	Sept.	Oct.	Nov.	Dec.	Total	$\div 12 =$ Average monthly expenses
____	____	____	____	____	____	____	_____
____	____	____	____	____	____	____	_____
____	____	____	____	____	____	____	_____
____	____	____	____	____	____	____	_____
____	____	____	____	____	____	____	_____
____	____	____	____	____	____	____	_____
____	____	____	____	____	____	____	_____
____	____	____	____	____	____	____	_____
____	____	____	____	____	____	____	_____
____	____	____	____	____	____	____	_____
____	____	____	____	____	____	____	_____
____	____	____	____	____	____	____	_____
____	____	____	____	____	____	____	_____
____	____	____	____	____	____	____	_____
____	____	____	____	____	____	____	_____
____	____	____	____	____	____	____	_____
____	____	____	____	____	____	____	_____
____	____	____	____	____	____	____	_____
____	____	____	____	____	____	____	_____

Worksheet III: Next Year's Estimated Expenses (Year: 19   )(Cont'd)

OTHER EXPENSE ITEMS	Jan.	Feb.	March	April	May	June
Subtotal	____	____	____	____	____	____
21. Food	____	____	____	____	____	____
22. Miscellaneous	____	____	____	____	____	____
23. Medical/dental/drugs	____	____	____	____	____	____
24. House repair	____	____	____	____	____	____
25. Clothing	____	____	____	____	____	____
26. Cleaning	____	____	____	____	____	____
27. Current Education	____	____	____	____	____	____
28. Auto repair and maintenance	____	____	____	____	____	____
29. Entertainment	____	____	____	____	____	____
30. Gifts	____	____	____	____	____	____
31. Travel	____	____	____	____	____	____
32. Other* _____	____	____	____	____	____	____
_____	____	____	____	____	____	____
_____	____	____	____	____	____	____
_____	____	____	____	____	____	____
Total monthly expenses	____	____	____	____	____	____
Total monthly income	____	____	____	____	____	____
Net surplus or deficit	____	____	____	____	____	____

* Including alimony and child support, pensions, union and professional dues, business expenses, church and charitable expenses, etc.

July	Aug.	Sept.	Oct.	Nov.	Dec.	Total	÷ 12 = Average monthly expenses
———	———	———	———	———	———	———	———
———	———	———	———	———	———	———	———
———	———	———	———	———	———	———	———
———	———	———	———	———	———	———	———
———	———	———	———	———	———	———	———
———	———	———	———	———	———	———	———
———	———	———	———	———	———	———	———
———	———	———	———	———	———	———	———
———	———	———	———	———	———	———	———
———	———	———	———	———	———	———	———
———	———	———	———	———	———	———	———
———	———	———	———	———	———	———	———
———	———	———	———	———	———	———	———
———	———	———	———	———	———	———	———
———	———	———	———	———	———	———	———
———	———	———	———	———	———	———	———
———	———	———	———	———	———	———	———
———	———	———	———	———	———	———	———

Chapter Nine

Implementing Your Financial Plan

Congratulations! By completing this book you have in effect prepared your own financial plan.

- You've analyzed your current financial situation.
- You've set your financial goals.
- And you've developed a budget to achieve them.

Now that you have a general plan, you will probably need advice and assistance from financial specialists to implement it.

Financial Specialists

Most people utilize certain financial specialists for advice and assistance, including accountants, attorneys, insurance representatives, and securities brokers. The ones you use become part of your financial "team."

Look back through this book and see in what areas you felt you needed advice and assistance. For example:

Legal. Review pages 4–5 about "Your Will." If you have any questions about your will or other legal questions, see your attorney.

Taxes. Review your "Tax Strategy Checklist" on page 33. Are there any ideas that you felt were worth pursuing, such as IRAs, gifts to minors, or municipal bonds? If so, consult the appropriate financial specialist. For questions about taxes you may want to see a qualified tax specialist, such as an accountant or attorney.

Insurance. Review your "Insurance Checklist" on page 57. Are there areas in which you felt your insurance coverage is possibly inadequate?

Did you have any questions? If so, your insurance representative will review your coverage with you at no charge and answer any questions. In general, life insurance representatives handle life and health insurance; property and casualty representatives handle auto and home insurance; and "multilines" representatives handle both.

Investments. Review your "Investment Checklist" on pages 70–72. Are there particular investments you felt were worth investigating? Or current investments that you might want to increase or decrease? If you have any questions, consult your securities broker or other qualified investment specialist. In today's financial marketplace, investment advice may be available from a wide range of sources, including some insurance representatives, some accountants, and some banks.

Choosing a Financial Specialist

If you do not already have a specialist in a particular field, ask your friends, relatives, and business associates for their recommendations. Contact professional organizations, such as your local bar association for an attorney or the American Society of CLU (Bryn Mawr, PA 19010) for an insurance representative. Or contact one or more firms which you believe to be sound and reputable. After you obtain some names, evaluate their credentials. Meet them to see if you feel comfortable with them. Pay attention to the soundness and reputation of the firm they represent. In short, select your specialists with care—they are key members of your financial team.

Compensation

Any time you seek financial advice and assistance from a specialist the specialist will, of course, have to be compensated for the time and effort involved. Accountants and attorneys are usually compensated on a fee basis, so you receive a bill for their services. Insurance representatives and securities brokers are usually compensated on a commission basis, so their fee is part of the price of any product you purchase. Even though you don't pay a specific fee, you are still paying for their advice and assistance if you make a purchase.

Financial Planners—A Word of Advice

A growing number of people today present themselves as financial planners or financial consultants. Some of them are superbly qualified professionals. Others have no visible qualifications at all.

Don't be misled! Even the best financial planner cannot replace *you* in the decision-making process. Only *you* know what you want to accomplish with your money. Only *you* can evaluate the alternatives and make the ultimate decisions. That's what this book is about.

What a financial planner offers is advice and assistance, just like your financial specialists. In fact, most financial planners are specialists in one financial area but who also have some expertise as generalists.

Who needs a financial planner? Financial planners vary greatly in the services they provide. As a general rule, the need for comprehensive financial planning advice tends to exist primarily in families that have reasonably large amounts of income, such as $50,000 a year or more, and substantial enough assets to justify the time and effort involved.

How do you choose a financial planner? The same way you choose a financial specialist: carefully. Ask for references from other persons who have used the services of the planner. Understand clearly what services will be provided and how the planner will be compensated. If the planner is associated with a firm, pay attention to the soundness and reputation of the firm he or she represents. Ask about qualifications such as the Chartered Financial Consultant (ChFC) or Chartered Life Underwriter (CLU) designations from the American College in Bryn Mawr, Pennsylvania, or the Certified Financial Planner (CFP) designation from the College for Financial Planning in Denver, Colorado. These designations, or study toward them, do not guarantee a good planner, but they do indicate a certain amount of technical knowledge. The American Institute of Certified Public Accountants also offers an education course for CPAs who want to become financial planners.

Who pays for financial planning? The cost of fee-based financial planning may run from several hundred to many thousands of dollars, depending on the person doing the planning and the complexity of your situation. Services provided for free indicate that the planner operates on a commission basis and hopes to be compensated by your purchase of financial products or use of financial services. There is nothing wrong with this and it can indeed be an advantage—as long as you are aware of it. If you use a planner, be sure you understand how your planner is compensated, and particularly whether he or she receives commissions for products or services provided.

Coordination

As you went through this book you probably noticed that many financial questions are related to each other.

- Your investment choices are affected by tax considerations.
- Your will and your life insurance are closely related since both affect the disposition of property at death. If your estate is large enough, tax questions will also have an impact on these areas.
- The kind of insurance coverage you have may allow you to take more risks and get by with less liquidity in your investments.
- Your budget, of course, is the central mechanism for coordinating most of these areas.

As you implement your plan by working with your financial specialists, you'll want to pay attention to how the various areas—tax, investment, and insurance—are related to each other. In most cases, there are compromises and trade-offs about which only you can decide. The ultimate decision is *always* up to you.

Monitoring

Even after you've implemented your financial plan, the job is not done. Financial planning is *never* done. Your financial situation changes constantly, so you need to constantly monitor it. Approximately once a year you should run through this entire book and see whether your financial plan is still on track.

- Is your will still appropriate for your needs?
- Have you saved as much money as you planned?
- Is your insurance coverage still adequate?
- Are there tax saving ideas you should consider?
- Are your investments still appropriate for your financial goals?

As usual, you should consult with your financial specialists, since they will have up-to-date information about legislative changes or new products in their areas of expertise.

Procrastination

One final word: The biggest problem in implementing a financial plan is procrastination. Many people know they ought to do something, but they put it off and put it off some more.

So—

Decide what you want to do,
Decide who you need to see, and
Make an appointment!

Once you make the appointment, you are setting the wheels in motion to implement your plan. The financial specialist or specialists you contact will then shoulder much of the responsibility for accomplishing your goals. They recognize that it is in your best interests to do so. So write down:

	NAME	PHONE #
Who you want to see	_____	_____
	_____	_____
	_____	_____
	_____	_____
	_____	_____

And call.

DO IT NOW!

Good luck!

The Prudential Insurance Company of America, with corporate headquarters in Newark, New Jersey, is the nation's largest insurance company.

For many years, the company has offered individual life insurance, health insurance, and annuities to consumers, and group life, health, and annuities to employers and other group clients. During the 1970s, the company diversified into the property and casualty field, offering auto and homeowners insurance through its agents. In 1981, it acquired Bache Halsey Stuart Shields, Inc., a securities brokerage firm that was subsequently renamed Prudential-Bache Securities, Inc.

Today, many of The Prudential's 23,000 insurance agents offer mutual funds and other investment products in addition to a full line of insurance products for life, health, auto, and home.

Katherine Barrett, editorial consultant for this book, serves as a contributing editor at the *Ladies' Home Journal* and co-author of the *Journal*'s personal finance column, "Money News." She has also written about personal finance and a variety of other topics for such national magazines as *Better Homes & Gardens, Family Circle, Seventeen, Harper's, Brides,* and *Family Weekly.*

Richard A. Mathisen, served as general editor of this book.

The Prudential welcomes your comments and suggestions about this book, especially those that might be used to improve any future editions. Please address your comments to:

The Prudential Insurance Company of America
P.O. Box 36
Newark, NJ 07101

Index